# NEW SWAN SHAKESPEARE

GENERAL EDITOR
BERNARD LOTT, M.A., PH. D.

## A Midsummer Night's Dream

NEW SWAN SHAKESPEARE

*Macbeth*

*Julius Caesar*

*Twelfth Night*

*Richard II*

*A Midsummer Night's Dream*

*The Merchant of Venice*

*Henry V*

*Romeo and Juliet*

*Henry IV, Part I*

*As You Like It*

WILLIAM SHAKESPEARE

# *A Midsummer Night's Dream*

EDITED BY
J. W. LEVER, M.A.

LONGMAN

**LONGMAN GROUP LIMITED**
London

*Associated companies, branches and representatives*
*throughout the world*

This edition © Longman Group Ltd. (formerly Longmans,
Green & Co. Ltd.) 1961, 1965

*First published 1961*
*Second edition \*1965*
*New impressions \*1966; \*1967; \*1968;*
*\*1969; \*1970; \*1974*

ISBN 0 582 52717 1

Illustrations by H. C. McBeath

We are indebted to the University of London for
permission to reproduce extracts from the English
Literature papers of the General Certificate of
Education, Ordinary Level.

*Printed in Hong Kong by*
*Peninsula Press Ltd.*

# GENERAL INTRODUCTION

The purpose of this book is to present a play by William Shakespeare in the simplest and most direct way. It is not a "simplified" text, nor an attempt to "tell the story" of *A Midsummer Night's Dream*. On the contrary, the text itself, which forms the greater part of the book, remains as the author wrote it (or as near to that ideal as we are now ever likely to come). Everything added has only one aim in view: to help the reader in his understanding of the play. He may very well need further help in getting greater pleasure out of the reading, for example by learning more about Shakespeare or about drama as an art. But his first duty is to understand the play and what the characters are saying; it is this purpose which has been kept in mind throughout the preparation of the book.

In order to make quite certain that the help given will in fact simplify the difficulties which are now found in so much of Shakespeare, and not just add more difficulties, explanations have been given within the range of a specially chosen list of 3,000 most commonly used English root-words. Every word in the book which falls outside this list is explained: words which are not used in Modern English as Shakespeare used them, or which are not now used at all, will be found explained in notes on the pages facing the text; words which are still used in Modern English, with their meanings unchanged, but which are not among the 3,000 root-words of the chosen list, will be found explained in the glossary at the back of the book. It is hoped that these explanations will be sufficiently clear and direct to remove all difficulties in the understanding of the text. Because of the changed use of idioms and expressions, whole passages are given longer explanation; this is also done within the range of the word-list.

A few words and expressions used in Shakespeare's time occur so frequently that there would be no gain in explaining them in the notes on each occasion. Their meanings are given here:

*anon* – "very soon".
*ay (aye)* – "yes".

*eke* – "also".

*ere* – "before" (with another word; *ere now*: "before now").

*forsooth* – "indeed".

*methinks (methought)* – "it seems (seemed) to me".

*nay* – "no".

*o'er* – "over".

*prithee* – "please" ("I pray thee").

*wont* – (n) "habit"; (v) *wont to (do, be,* etc.) "in the habit (of doing, being)".

*yea* – "yes".

*Thou, thee* (as object) were commonly used between friends instead of "you". Some verb forms with *thou* are: *art* (are), *wilt* (will), *shalt* (shall), *hast* (have), and generally *-st* as an ending to the verb root.

In the "Introduction to this Play" which follows, there is first a note on the nature of the play and then a closer study of the play under these headings:

# INTRODUCTION TO THIS PLAY

*A Midsummer Night's Dream* was written about 1595 as an entertainment at the marriage of some great nobleman, and was later performed in the public theatre. Shakespeare was still young, and this is one of his gayest and happiest plays, with its songs and dances, beautiful poetry, clever ideas and simple fun. Many kinds of amusement are mixed in just the right proportion: there is love-making and laughter, nonsense and very good sense. But to enjoy the play we must approach it in the proper way. An entertainment of this kind is meant to appeal to our imagination, not our interest in facts. It does not tell a true story or describe real historical events. The audience who watched this play delighted in hearing the ancient Greek stories of the adventures of gods and goddesses, great kings and beautiful queens. Accordingly there is mention of Diana the moon goddess, Cupid the love god, Hercules, Helen, and other famous figures. The two chief characters at the beginning and end are Theseus and Hippolyta, persons about whom stories and poems have been written, but who may never have existed at all. The events in the play are supposed to have happened in or near Athens, but Athens as described here is not the real place, ancient or modern; it is rather a "country of the mind", where all kinds of strange adventures seem possible. Similarly, Englishmen in the time of Elizabeth I liked to hear the old stories of their own land about fairies, elves and goblins – imaginary creatures who lived in the woods and fields. Hence we find that in this play there are woods round Athens (although the real Athens is far from any forest) and that in the woods Oberon and Titania, king and queen of the fairies, hold their court. As for the happenings in Acts II to IV, where magic plays so large a part, these are as imaginary as the forest and its fairies. They are meant to please and amuse us, not to teach us history. Yet by the time we have finished, we discover that Shakespeare has, after all, told the truth, not about particular persons and events, but about the way human beings in general think, act and love.

This is only an outline so that the general design of the play may be considered. At the beginning of each scene an account has been given of the chief happenings in that scene.

The story is supposed to take place in ancient times. Theseus, Duke of Athens, and Hippolyta, Queen of the Amazons, are about to be married. An old man named Egeus comes to Theseus and asks him to force Hermia, the daughter of Egeus, to marry the young Demetrius. Hermia has refused because she is in love with another young man, Lysander. As for Demetrius, who now wishes to marry Hermia, he has broken his earlier promise to marry Helena, Hermia's friend since their schooldays, who still loves him. Theseus gives Hermia time to think it over until the day of his own marriage. But meanwhile Hermia and Lysander plan secretly to escape through the woods. Demetrius hears of this plan. He decides to follow them and Helena decides to follow him.

A group of working men in Athens, of whom Bottom the weaver is the most active and talkative, wishes to perform a play at the court of Theseus in honour of his marriage, and decides to practise in the woods.

In these woods live the fairies. Their king and queen, Oberon and Titania, have quarrelled; as a result the weather is upset and the crops are spoiled. Oberon calls Puck (or Robin Goodfellow), a spirit who likes to play tricks on people, and orders him to pick a magic flower. Its juice, put on the eyes of a sleeping person, makes that person fall madly in love with the first living thing he or she sees on waking up. Oberon hopes in this way to bewitch Titania and punish her.

Lysander and Hermia, Demetrius and Helena all come to the woods at night. So do Bottom and his companions. Through Puck's mistakes, some very complicated misunderstandings are brought about. The queen of the fairies falls in love with Bottom, who has been bewitched by Puck so that he has the head of a donkey. Lysander and Demetrius, who had been rivals for Hermia, now give her up and become rivals for Helena instead. The two girls quarrel. These confusions go on all through the night until, just before sunrise, Oberon takes off the magic charm. Bottom gets his own head back; Oberon and Titania put an end to their quarrel.

When Theseus and Hippolyta come through the woods hunting next morning, they find and wake up the sleeping lovers. All is well again. Lysander and Hermia are united in love, and so are Demetrius and Helena.

Back in Athens, Theseus and Hippolyta celebrate their marriage, and the two pairs of lovers are married at the same time as their rulers. Egeus has been ordered to agree to this and there is general rejoicing. Bottom and his companions act their play before the ladies and gentlemen, much to everyone's amusement. At the end, Oberon and Titania, with their fairies and elves, come to dance, sing and bless the marriage, while Puck stays to sweep the palace.

Even from this short account it will be seen how cleverly these quite different groups of people are brought together and their adventures made into a pattern. The groups are (i) the young lovers; (ii) the ordinary working men; (iii) the fairies. At first we are introduced to them separately, group by group. Then in the wood, as a result of Puck's magic, they come into contact with one another in a set of misunderstandings which become ever wilder and more laughable. Lastly, all three groups are brought into harmony under the wise authority of Theseus and Hippolyta, so that love and happiness prevail.

But in a good play the interest lies in more qualities than just a cleverly made pattern of events. There are the characters themselves, and their way of acting and thinking. There are the different forms through which they express themselves, in verse and prose. Most important, perhaps, is the total effect the play has on our minds; the shaping of our sympathies in such matters as love, marriage and loyalty with which the play is concerned. For while there is much to laugh at in *A Midsummer Night's Dream,* and much beauty to enjoy, there is also a serious view of life and human behaviour which gradually reveals itself.

## 2 The Characters

(i) *The Lovers.* Lysander and Demetrius, Hermia and Helena, are not very distinct as individuals. There are small differences, of course. Lysander, until he is bewitched, seems a more steady and sincere person than Demetrius, whose vows to Helena were so soon forgotten. Hermia is short in height, dark, and more excitable than the tall, fair and rather gentle Helena. In the midst of their quarrel in III.ii, it is Hermia who threatens to attack, and Helena who runs away. But more important than such differences is their similarity as a group. All four are young, good-looking, and in love. They are well-educated, well-spoken and trained in polite manners. Theseus and Hippolyta welcome them to be married at the royal wedding, and are glad to have their company afterwards at the play. What these lovers lack is the wisdom and experience that Theseus and Hippolyta possess. They have strong feelings but not much power of judgement, and nothing brings this out more clearly than their behaviour when Puck has bewitched them. Their sudden changes of affection, and the way the young men address exactly the same excessive praise and the same vows of eternal love to Helena as they had done before so Hermia, show that they are not yet really grown up. We laugh at them, and even pity them, rather than blame them. And much of the amusement arises from the fact that they are so much alike. They are types of young lovers everywhere, although they speak and behave in the style which was fashionable in the Elizabethan age.

(ii) *The Working-men.* These, too, are types rather than individuals, though Bottom stands out from the rest. We think of them by their trades – "Starveling the tailor", "Snug the joiner", "Bottom the weaver", etc; and their very names would suggest their trades to an Elizabethan audience (see note 1 to I.ii). Quince the carpenter organizes the others and settles their parts in the play. Bottom is the most talkative and the readiest to offer himself for any part. Snug is "slow of study", and has little to say. Flute, who is chosen to play Thisbe, is still a boy. They are all simple, uneducated people, "hempen home-spuns" as Puck calls them, who misuse words, have little imagination when it comes to producing the play, and yet are so superstitious that they run away in fear when Puck performs his magic. Although described as tradesmen of ancient Athens, they are not in the least like the clever, lively Athenians we find in old Greek plays. In reality they are much more like the ordinary village people of Shakespeare's time, ignorant but good-tempered, very respectful to the ladies and gentlemen of the court, and with a great desire to please their ruler.

Bottom is no better educated than the rest, but has a great deal more self-confidence. He is quite sure that he will be a success in any part he takes in the play. Cheerful and talkative (though misusing his words worse than the others), he has very little fear of anybody or anything. Even when he is bewitched and becomes the lover of the fairy queen, he behaves confidently, making friends with the fairy attendants and accepting calmly the benefits that come to him. In the part of Pyramus, he twice turns to correct the Duke about how the play should be acted, the second time getting up from the ground where he is supposed to be dead. Yet even Bottom, when he remembers his adventures in fairy-land, feels that he has had "a most rare vision". Something strange and wonderful has entered into his life.

(iii) *The Fairies.* Most country people in all lands have old, superstitious beliefs about spirits who help or harm the crops, control the weather, and make young children healthy or weak. The people of Britain called these spirits "fairies" or "elves". They were supposed to live in the woods, though they would come out into the fields at night to dance in a ring. If annoyed they could do much harm, but if treated kindly they would guard small children and even help with the housework. Goblins, called "the Puck" or "Robin Goodfellow", were rather different. They were ugly, hairy and very fond of mischief, but they, too, could learn to be good and helpful. All these spirits were very small; in Ireland they are still called the "little people".

Shakespeare must have had children to act the parts of the fairies, and they add a lot to the entertainment by their songs, dances, and poetic descriptions of country life. The fairies are imagined as having a king, queen and court of their own, with guards like Queen Elizabeth's "gentlemen pensioners", and elves as servants, like her "ladies in waiting". But unlike wise human rulers, Oberon and Titania are completely under the influence of their feelings. Love, anger, jealousy are very quickly stirred up in them. They have very little control over their actions. At the beginning of the play they have quarrelled about "a lovely boy stolen from an Indian king", and this quarrel is given as the reason why the weather is upset and the whole country flooded in summer time. It is very necessary that the kingdom of the fairies should be set in order if things are to go well with human beings. At the end, when Oberon and Titania are friends again, these fairy rulers come to bless Theseus and Hippolyta. They promise that there will be happiness for all the human lovers and the children of their marriages.

Puck is the liveliest spirit of them all. He can move with almost lightning speed, "swifter than arrow from the Tartar's bow", travelling round the earth in forty minutes. Some of the tricks he plays on the village people are described in II.i.34–57. Although the confusion he brings about with the magic flower is not intentional but due to a mistake, he finds much fun in the lovers' strange behaviour. "Lord, what fools these mortals be!" he exclaims. The bewitching of Bottom and chasing away of Bottom's companions is all his own idea, which he afterwards reports to Oberon with great delight. Yet in the end even Puck has been tamed. He appears with a broom to sweep away the dust behind the palace door, as a good household servant of Theseus and Hippolyta, and in the last lines of the play he speaks to the audience as their friend.

(iv) *Theseus and Hippolyta.* These two are presented as model lovers and model rulers, setting an example of wise and fair behaviour to all their people. They are not young and excitable, like the four lovers; they have lived through many experiences before the time comes for them to marry. Theseus does not entirely support the demand of Egeus that his daughter Hermia should be forced to obey her father. But it is plain that Hermia and the other young persons have much to learn about their own feelings, and therefore Theseus decides that the case shall be postponed a little time so that they can make up their minds. When he finds them asleep in the woods next morning, he insists that Egeus should give way and let the lovers, who have grown up through the experiences of the night, marry as they choose.

As rulers, Theseus and Hippolyta clearly have the affection of their people. Bottom and his friends gladly prepare a play to do them honour, and everyone speaks of them with respect. But Theseus also knows that a good ruler will show politeness in return and take an interest in his people. Although "Pyramus and Thisbe" is a very foolish play and very badly acted, Theseus is careful not to laugh at the performance. He makes Hippolyta and the rest of the court behave as he does, and praises the actors for the trouble they have taken.

Theseus and Hippolyta appear only at the beginning and towards the end of the play. They have no share in the adventures that happen to the lovers or to Bottom and his companions in the woods, for indeed *their* adventures are over before the play begins. Instead, they represent a kind of permanence and order in life and society, which stands out clearly against the changes and confusion experienced by all the other characters.

## 3 *Construction and Ideas*

These groups are brought together, as we have seen, by the clever planning of the story. For various reasons the characters meet in the woods, where the human beings come under the influence of the fairies through Puck's magic. But it is not only the story which links them together. If we look more closely we find that the different groups have much more in common than appears at first. The lovers, it has been said, speak and think like well-educated young ladies and gentlemen in Elizabethan England. Bottom, Quince, Snug and the rest, though described as Athenians, are very like the simpler types of country people whom Shakespeare knew as a boy. The fairies and Puck are, of course, imaginary beings; but their talk is full of descriptions of real English country life – the plants and flowers that grow in the summer, the little creatures in the woods and fields, the work and games of the country people. Since the fairies, elves and goblins existed in the imaginations of countrymen, it might be said that they, too, belong to the life of that time. Lastly, even Theseus and Hippolyta behave more like the great nobles of Queen Elizabeth's reign than like Dukes and Duchesses of ancient Athens, and their gracious treatment of Bottom and his friends follows the best example set by the queen and her court when visiting the towns and big country-houses of England.

What we find, then, is that these groups, seemingly so different, in reality represent various levels of English society in Shakespeare's time. At the marriage of a great Elizabethan nobleman, all these would be found taking part in the celebrations. Young ladies and gentlemen, like Lysander and Demetrius, Hermia and Helena, would be invited to the feast from all the districts around. The simple country people who lived on the estate would come to show their respect, and would usually provide some kind of entertainment

– as do Bottom and his companions – in the form of a dance or play. Quite commonly the old stories and beliefs of the countryside would be acted or told in verse. The great house of the nobleman's family (not much smaller than some palaces) would be lit up at night, the grounds would be open to all comers, and when the marriage was completed, everyone rejoiced in the hope that a healthy and wise heir would be born to take over the estate some day and look after it for the general good.

Shakespeare's play was performed as an entertainment for one such celebration. Its characters are drawn from the same types as the people present, and its ideas are of the kind that would be thought of at such a time. Since the ancient poetry of Greece and Rome was well known to educated persons, and since Shakespeare himself loved it, the story is supposed to happen in Athens, the main characters have Greek names, and all through the play there is mention of the deeds of ancient gods and heroes. But its chief interest lies in the way it presents life and love in Elizabethan England. Here is a picture of a happy country society, united under a model ruler. Theseus and Hippolyta represent, in ideal form, the noble pair for whose marriage in real life the play was written. Even more important than these great persons was their royal mistress, Queen Elizabeth I. She may have been present when, in II.i, Oberon speaks of "the imperial votaress. . . . In maiden meditation, fancy free". Whether the queen actually heard these words, everybody in the audience would understand that they referred to her. She would come into their minds at that moment as the leader of the whole nation to whom everybody's loyalty was due.

Here, too, expressed through the events of the play, is Shakespeare's view of love in a well ordered society. While old people should be respected, it is not good for them to force their children into marrying against their will. But for young lovers to be happy, a process of growing up is necessary. They must choose wisely, following the example of Theseus and Hippolyta. Love which exists only in the imagination is blind: nothing shows this more plainly than the wild confusion brought about in the woods. There the four lovers lose all power of calm reasoning, and let their passions and jealousies rage on without control. They have become more like the fairies than like responsible human beings. No wonder that

Theseus in V.i.8 describes "The lunatic, the lover and the poet" as composed entirely of imagination. Yet when the lovers awaken next morning, they are changed. It is as if they had lived through all the foolishness of youth in one night, and grown up into thoughtful men and women. Demetrius now knows that he truly loves Helena, and the love between Lysander and Hermia has become more deep and sincere.

Reason is necessary if love is to succeed, just as wise rulers are necessary if society is to stay united. But reason alone is not sufficient for human beings; nature, too, must work with it. It is the fairies who represent nature in this play, as well as being the forces of imagination through which nature is understood. It is right, therefore, that the fairies should come back at the end of the play, tame now and loyal to Theseus and the force of reason which he represents. They will give their blessings to the newly married lovers –

> So shall all the couples three
> Ever true in loving be    (V.i.386-7)

– and preserve their children from harm.

In a way, these ideas are brought out, too, in the story of Bottom and his friends. As simple and rather stupid people, they lack both reason and imagination. Much of the amusement comes from their ignorance of how a play can be produced; how moonlight, for example, can be brought to mind by poetry without any need for a man to come in carrying a lamp and pretending to be the moon. They choose a play with a sad subject, about the bad fortune and death of young lovers (rather like the story of Shakespeare's *Romeo and Juliet*); but they have so little imagination that their acting moves the audience to laughter instead of tears. Yet for Bottom at least, the cleverest of them all, the night in the woods brings a real adventure. He is chosen by the fairy queen, and finds himself, if only for a short time, in a world of beauty and love. Next day he and his friends act before the ladies and gentlemen; they have realized their ambition, and receive praise from the Duke. Although these men's minds are limited to everyday matters, they are honest, loyal and hard-working. It is good and right that these qualities should be honoured in society together with the forces of reason and imagination represented by Theseus and the fairies.

## 4 *The Language of the Play*

Just as there is much variety in the groups of characters and their way of seeing life, so there is variety of expression. *A Midsummer Night's Dream* is not written all in one style. Each group has a typical way of speaking which is specially suited to it. Theseus and Hippolyta express themselves in "blank verse", a kind of verse without rhyme but having five clear beats in each line. For example:

> For yóu, fair Hérmia, lóok you árm yoursélf
> To fít your fáncies tó your fáther's wíll;
> Or élse the láw of Áthens yiélds you úp –
> Whích by no méans we máy exténuáte –
> To déath, or tó a vów of síngle lífe. (I.i.118-22).

The effect is sensible and dignified, as if we were listening to a wise, clear-thinking person who has carefully considered his words. Sometimes the lovers speak blank verse, especially when they are with older people, but when they are by themselves they often change to "rhyming couplets", where each pair of lines has a rhyme of its own:

*Hermia:* What love could press Lysander from my side?
*Lysander:* Lysander's love, that would not let him bide;
              Fair Helena, who more engilds the night
              Than all yon fiery oes and eyes of light. (III.ii.185-8)

The effect is more graceful and pleasing to the ear, but we pay less heed to the thought than we do in the blank verse speeches. This is quite in keeping with the way we regard the lovers through most of the play: their feelings are more noticeable than their ideas. Usually the fairies speak in rhyme, though Oberon and Titania, being more dignified figures than the rest, may use blank verse. Often we find a light, skipping kind of poetry, made up of short, rhyming lines, which expresses the character of these gay, quick-moving creatures; for instance:

> Over hill, over dale,
> Thorough brush, thorough brier,
> Over park, over pale,
> Thorough flood, thorough fire, etc. (II.i.2-5).

Sometimes the fairy verse turns into song, as in "You spotted snakes", II.ii.9; or there may even be a song and dance without any words (see note 195 to V.i). Lastly, Bottom and his companions speak prose. They are ordinary, practical people, for whom everyday language is the most fitting. When, in "Pyramus and Thisbe", they act their parts in verse, this is so badly spoken that the audience cannot help laughing.

## 5 Imagery

Much of the force of Shakespeare's play lies in its use of imagery: that is, in the way a thing or person is connected in idea with something or someone else. For example, Helena describes her long friendship with Hermia:

> So we grew together,
> Like to a double cherry, seeming parted,
> But yet an union in partition. (III.ii.208–10)

This image of the double cherry does more than just repeat the statement that the two girls were close friends. It also leads us to think of them in connection with beautiful things in nature that grow and ripen; and this in turn shapes our attitude to Helena, Hermia and their problems of growing up, making us see these as part of a natural process for plants and human beings alike. When a direct comparison is made, using the word "as" or "like", the image is called a *simile*. Sometimes, however, the image makes no use of such words of comparison, and suggests that the thing spoken of and the thing it is said to be like are actually one and the same; as when Lysander asks Hermia:

> Why is your cheek so pale?
> How chance the roses there do fade so fast? (I.i.129–30)

Here the rose image is expressed as if Hermia's cheek really *was* a garden in which roses grew. Images of this kind are called *metaphors*. And here too we are made to think, not only of the simple resemblance between beautiful girls and beautiful flowers, but of other qualities, too, which they have in common, qualities such as Theseus had already described in lines 75–79 of the same scene. One image connects with another, forming a pattern of ideas, and this adds a richness of thought and feeling to the whole impression.

Fashions change in poetry as well as in clothes. When Shakespeare was young, love poetry had a set of words and images that appeared again and again. The lady was called a goddess or a nymph; her eyes were like stars; her cheeks like roses; her skin like snow. Her lover declared that he worshipped her for her beauty and virtue: he made vows to serve her and obey all her commands. In modern times this sounds artificial, and indeed Shakespeare himself thought it could be overdone. He makes his lovers speak in the fashionable style, but shows that it is more a habit than a sincere expression of feeling. When, under the influence of the magic, Demetrius wakes up to see Helena, whom he has scorned before, he at once pours out this kind of language:

> O Helen, goddess, nymph, perfect, divine,
> To what, my love, shall I compare thine eyne?
> Crystal is muddy; O how ripe in show
> Thy lips, those kissing cherries, tempting grow! (III.ii.137–40)

We are not intended to take this seriously: it is part of the fun of the play, and the style is laughed at when "Thisbe" describes "Pyramus" with the same images, but wrongly applied:

> These lily lips,
> This cherry nose,
>   These yellow cowslip cheeks,
> Are gone, are gone:
> Lovers, make moan:
>   His eyes were green as leeks (V.i.313–18).

Another fashion was to use imagery taken from the literature of ancient Greece and Rome. Modern readers are not so familiar with this literature as were the Elizabethans, and the mention of old gods and goddesses, rulers and great lovers, now seems strange. But writers today will mention characters in Shakespeare or Dickens, even though such writers may not be British or speak English as their own language. Since *A Midsummer Night's Dream* is supposed to take place in ancient Athens, the descriptions and images are quite suitable, and when one understands them, they are beautiful as well.

What is most striking, and typical of Shakespeare, is the way he fills this play with memories of the English countryside. The descriptions are so fresh and lively that every reader can enjoy them. There is mention of the old country women drinking their beer in winter, and of the great floods in midsummer (II.i.47–50; 88–111); of the birds flying across the sky after a gun has been fired (III.ii 20–23); of the hunting dogs with their musical cries (IV.i.108–20). The little fairies in their speeches remind us of the small flowers and wild creatures in the woods and fields. Titania's guards are the cowslips, with their gold, red-spotted coats. She sleeps on "a bank where the wild thyme grows", roofed over with woodbine, musk-roses and eglantine; her fairies fight against "rere mice" or bats, and keep away the snakes and hedgehogs, spiders and beetles. When Bottom is bewitched, he asks a fairy to kill "a red-hipped humble bee on top of a thistle", and Titania offers to send another fairy for fresh nuts saved up by the squirrel. These fairy attendants by their very names – Peaseblossom, Cobweb, Moth and Mustardseed – make us think of the sights of the country. In some ways the most imaginative parts of the play are the most real and true to nature.

One powerful image keeps appearing from the first lines of the play until almost the end. It is of the moon, which gives a beauty and dream-like quality to all it shines on. Theseus and Hippolyta are waiting for the new moon that will rise on their marriage night "like to a silver bow New bent in heaven" (I.i.9–10). In the same scene the lovers plan to meet in the woods after midnight when the old moon has risen, "Decking with liquid pearl the bladed grass" (I.i.212). The moon shines for Oberon and Titania who are "ill met by moonlight" (II.i.60), and through the following scenes the frequent mention of moonlight keeps it in our thoughts. There was no artificial lighting in the theatre when *A Midsummer Night's Dream* was first performed: all these descriptions were meant to help us to imagine the woods at night through the poetry instead of the scenery. About the middle of III.ii., we notice that the characters have stopped speaking of the moon. The night is much darker too, and Lysander points to "yon fiery oes and eyes of light" (III.ii.188) – the stars which continue to shine when the moon has set. Later still, "Aurora's harbinger" (the star which appears before sunrise) is seen by Puck (line 380), and just before the fairies leave, Puck hears the morning lark (IV.i.90). A minute or two later there is the loud sound of horns; Theseus and Hippolyta with their followers enter dressed for hunting. The day has begun, and night with its dreams and magic is over. But in the last act of the play it is night again, the night of happy marriages. An artificial moon is provided by Starveling with his lamp during the performance of "Pyramus and Thisbe"; and after the entertainment is over, when all the human beings have gone to bed, Puck enters to describe the midnight time, with the real moon shining and the fairies "Following darkness like a dream" (V.i.365). Dreams and magic have returned to the world, bringing their blessing to the newly married; and the moon is their sign.

## 6 *A Midsummer Night's Dream in the Theatre*

Besides being shown as a private entertainment, this play was publicly performed in the theatre. The stage in Elizabethan times had no front curtain and very little scenery. Women's parts were acted by boys, and the plays were put on in the afternoon. But the poetry, songs and dances greatly helped the audience to imagine the woods at night, the moonlight, stars and magic. In this play, too, much use would be made of the "inner stage", which was a small room at the back of the main stage that could be shut off by a curtain (or screen). Here a bank of flowers would be arranged to make Titania's sleeping-place in II.ii, and in III.1 Bottom retires behind the screen, to come back wearing the donkey's head. Titania and her fairies will take him in there at the end of the scene, and with the curtain drawn again, the main stage will become "another part of the wood" for III.ii. At the beginning of Act IV, while the lovers are asleep, Titania and Bottom will come in and sit down together on the same "bank" of the inner stage, where they, too, fall asleep until Oberon comes forward to call Titania. In Act V, with the inner stage closed off, the main stage will become the palace of Theseus, as it was in Act I; but towards the end Puck will enter through the curtain, and Oberon and Titania may go back through it, leaving Puck to speak the last words before he, too, retires.

It is quite easy to act *A Midsummer Night's Dream* in the way Shakespeare intended it. The play can be performed in a garden, or in any school hall with a few plants or flowers that can be quickly put on and taken away. The main stage need not have a curtain, but some kind of curtain or screen should be used to cover or reveal

Titania's sleeping-place. Boys can act the parts of women – as they did in Elizabethan times – or girls the parts of men; and younger children should act as fairies. Bright and pleasant clothes are important, but these do not have to be Elizabethan. The old-style clothes worn by ladies and gentlemen, following the custom of the country where the play is performed, will do as well; Bottom and his friends may be dressed as workmen; and the fairies may look like spirits as imagined by the simple people of the country. Complicated scenery and lighting are not at all necessary. If the songs, dances and music are good, the actors well dressed and the speeches clearly pronounced, the imagination of the audience should supply the rest. At any rate, that is what Shakespeare wanted it to do.

# DRAMATIS PERSONAE

THESEUS, *Duke of Athens*

EGEUS, *father of Hermia*

LYSANDER }
DEMETRIUS } *in love with Hermia*

PHILOSTRATE, *provider of the Duke's entertainments*

QUINCE, *a carpenter*

SNUG, *a joiner*

BOTTOM, *a weaver*

FLUTE, *a bellows-mender*

SNOUT, *a tinker*

STARVELING, *a tailor*

HIPPOLYTA, *Queen of the Amazons, a nation of women fighters, betrothed to Theseus*

HERMIA, *daughter of Egeus, in love with Lysander*

HELENA, *in love with Demetrius*

OBERON, *King of the Fairies*

TITANIA, *Queen of the Fairies*

PUCK, *or* ROBIN GOODFELLOW, *a spirit of mischief*

PEASEBLOSSOM
COBWEB
MOTH }
MUSTARDSEED } *fairies*

(1.i) Theseus and Hippolyta arrange for their wedding at the coming of the new moon. Egeus enters with a complaint. His daughter Hermia refuses to marry Demetrius, whom Egeus has chosen to be her husband, because she is in love with Lysander. Theseus orders Hermia to choose before the next new moon: either to obey her father, or to suffer death, or to stay single for life. Lysander and Hermia make plans to meet secretly in the wood outside Athens and escape. Helena learns of their plan. She is in love with Demetrius, who scorns her. She decides to tell Demetrius about Hermia's flight in order to gain his favour.

1 *our nuptial hour* – "the time for our wedding".

2 *Draws on apace* – "approaches rapidly (*apace*)".

3 *lingers* – "delays".

4 *step-dame* – "step-mother" (one's father's second wife).

5 *a dowager . . . revenue* – "the widow of a rich husband (*dowager*), who lives long, using up (*withering out*) the money from the estate which, when she dies, will belong to the young heir".

6 *steep themselves in night* – "plunge into night". The idea is of day plunging into night's darkness as if into deep water.

7 *like to . . . heaven* – the new moon being shaped like a bent bow.

8 *pert and nimble* – "quick in mind (*pert*) and body (*nimble*)".

9 *turn melancholy forth to funerals* – "send melancholy off to funerals" (and not to a wedding).

10 *The pale . . . pomp.* Melancholy, imagined as a pale-faced guest, is not wanted at the wedding ceremony (*pomp*).

11 *I wooed thee with my sword* – "I won you as my wife by fighting against you".

12 *in another key* – "in a different style".

13 *pomp* – "splendid ceremony".

14 *triumph* – "stately processions".

# ACT ONE

## Scene I. Athens.

*Enter* THESEUS, HIPPOLYTA, PHILOSTRATE, *and* ATTENDANTS.

THESEUS

Now, fair Hippolyta, our nuptial hour[1]
Draws on apace:[2] four happy days bring in
Another moon: but O, methinks how slow
This old moon wanes; she lingers[3] my desires
Like to a step-dame,[4] or a dowager,                      5
Long withering out a young man's revenue.[5]

HIPPOLYTA

Four days will quickly steep themselves in night;[6]
Four nights will quickly dream away the time;
And then the moon, like to a silver bow
New bent in heaven,[7] shall behold the night          10
Of our solemnities.

THESEUS

Go, Philostrate,
Stir up the Athenian youth to merriments;
Awake the pert and nimble[8] spirit of mirth;
Turn melancholy forth to funerals:[9]                      15
The pale companion is not for our pomp.[10]

[*Exit* PHILOSTRATE

Hippolyta, I wooed thee with my sword,[11]
And won thy love doing thee injuries;
But I will wed thee in another key,[12]
With pomp,[13] with triumph,[14] and with revelling.   20

*Enter* EGEUS *and his daughter* HERMIA, LYSANDER, *and*
DEMETRIUS.

1

15 *Stand forth* – "Stand forward", "To the front".
16 *bewitched the bosom of my child* – "gained my child's love as if by witchcraft".
17. *rhymes* – "poems (of love)."
18 *interchanged love-tokens* – "exchanged gifts as signs of love".
19 *stolen . . . fantasy* – "secretly made a mark (*impression*) upon her thoughts".
20 *gawds* – "pretty ornaments of small value".

21 *conceits* – "curious little presents".
22 *knacks* – "small articles of dress".
23 *messengers of strong prevailment* – "carrying the message of love very persuasively".
24 *Be it so* – "If it be true that".
25 *I beg . . . Athens* – "I ask to use the ancient right (of a father) in Athens".
26 *dispose of her* – "get rid of her".
27 *Immediately* – "Directly"; "In so many words".

EGEUS

Happy be Theseus, our renownéd Duke!

THESEUS

Thanks, good Egeus: what's the news with thee?

EGEUS

Full of vexation come I, with complaint
Against my child, my daughter Hermia.
Stand forth,[15] Demetrius. My noble lord,
This man hath my consent to marry her.
Stand forth,[15] Lysander; and, my gracious Duke,
This man hath bewitched the bosom of my child:[16]
Thou, thou Lysander, thou hast given her rhymes,[17]
And interchanged love-tokens[18] with my child:
Thou hast by moonlight at her window sung,
With feigning voice, verses of feigning love,
And stolen the impression of her fantasy[19]
With bracelets of thy hair, rings, gawds,[20] conceits,[21]
Knacks,[22] trifles, nosegays, sweetmeats, messengers
Of strong prevailment[23] in unhardened youth;
With cunning hast thou filched my daughter's heart,
Turned her obedience, which is due to me,
To stubborn harshness. And, my gracious Duke,
Be it so[24] she will not here before your Grace
Consent to marry with Demetrius,
I beg the ancient privilege of Athens;[25]
As she is mine, I may dispose of her;[26]
Which shall be either to this gentleman,
Or to her death, according to our law
Immediately[27] provided in that case.

3

_father's right_

25

30

35

40

45

28 *be advised* – "take advice"; "be careful".

29 *composed* – "created", "gave shape to".

30 *as a form . . . imprinted* – "like a figure of wax which he (your father) has cut into shape (*imprinted*)".

31 *or disfigure it* – "or to destroy this figure".

32 *in this kind* – "in this matter".

33 *wanting . . . voice* – "lacking (*wanting*) your father's words of support".

34 *held* – "considered".

35 *would* – "wish".

36 *with his judgement look* – "look (upon these young men) in the way your father would judge them".

37 *concern* – "fit with".

38 *In such a presence* – i.e., of the Duke.

39 *to plead my thoughts* – "to argue for what I think right".

40 *die the death* – "be punished with death".

41 *society* – "company".

42 *question your desires* – "find out what you truly desire".

43 *Know of . . . blood* – "Know that you are only young; consider carefully your natural feelings (*blood*), (and decide)".

THESEUS

What say you, Hermia? be advised,[28] fair maid.
To you your father should be as a god;
One that composed[29] your beauties; yea, and one
To whom you are but as a form in wax
By him imprinted;[30] and within his power
To leave the figure, or disfigure it.[31]
Demetrius is a worthy gentleman.

HERMIA

So is Lysander.

THESEUS

In himself he is;
But in this kind,[32] wanting your father's voice,[33]                    55
The other must be held[34] the worthier.

HERMIA

I would[35] my father looked but with my eyes.

THESEUS

Rather your eyes must with his judgement look.[36]

HERMIA

I do entreat your Grace to pardon me.
I know not by what power I am made bold,                    60
Nor how it may concern[37] my modesty
In such a presence[38] here to plead my thoughts;[39]
But I beseech your Grace, that I may know
The worst that may befall me in this case,
If I refuse to wed Demetrius.                    65

THESEUS

Either to die the death,[40] or to abjure
For ever the society[41] of men.
Therefore, fair Hermia, question your desires,[42]
Know of your youth, examine well your blood,[43]

5

44 *endure the livery of a nun* – "bear having to wear the garments of a nun (q.v.)".

45 *For aye* – "For ever".

46 *mewed* – "shut in" (the word carries the idea of shutting up birds in a cage).

47 *sister* – "nun" (q.v.).

48 *Chanting . . . fruitless moon* – Although Theseus at times seems to be describing the life of a Catholic nun, the story is set in ancient Greece, where virgin priestesses worshipped the moon.

49 *master so their blood* – "so rule over their passions".

50 *undergo* – "take up", "endure".

51 *maiden pilgrimage* – "life of a virgin"; (*pilgrimage* stands here for life, considered as a journey that God calls on us to take).

52 *earthlier happy* – "happier upon the earth".

53 *the rose distilled* – "the rose whose scent is drawn from it and preserved". The idea is of a woman who marries and has children: these, like scent that remains after the flower has withered, preserve in themselves their mother's beauty when she is old.

54 *withering on the virgin thorn* – the rose that is not picked for scent and withers on its tree, i.e. the virgin who grows old.

55 *virgin patent* – "rights as a virgin".

56 *Unto his . . . sovereignty* – "To the mastery (*lordship*) of a man whose rule (*yoke*) my deepest feelings (*soul*) refuse to obey (*give sovereignty*)".

57 *The sealing-day* – "The day when the promise becomes binding" (like a bond that is sealed); i.e. the wedding day.

58 *as he would* – "as he (your father) wishes".

59 *Diana*. Virgin goddess of the moon and forests in the Greek religion.

60 *protest* – "declare in public (that one will keep)".

61 *crazed title* – "weak claim".

*You can endure the livery of a nun* [44]

6

Whether, if you yield not your father's choice,                          70
You can endure the livery of a nun,[44]
For aye[45] to be in shady cloister mewed,[46]
To live a barren sister[47] all your life,
Chanting faint hymns to the cold fruitless moon.[48]
Thrice blesséd they that master so their blood[49]                       75
To undergo[50] such maiden pilgrimage;[51]
But earthlier happy[52] is the rose distilled[53]
Than that which, withering on the virgin thorn,[54]
Grows, lives, and dies in single blessedness.

### HERMIA

So will I grow, so live, so die, my Lord,                                80
Ere I will yield my virgin patent[55] up
Unto his lordship, whose unwishéd yoke,
My soul consents not to give sovereignty.[56]

### THESEUS

Take time to pause, and by the next new moon,
The sealing-day[57] betwixt my love and me                              85
For everlasting bond of fellowship,
Upon that day either prepare to die
For disobedience to your father's will,
Or else to wed Demetrius as he would,[58]
Or on Diana's[59] altar to protest[60]                                  90
For aye austerity and single life.

### DEMETRIUS

Relent, sweet Hermia, and Lysander, yield
Thy crazéd title[61] to my certain right.

### LYSANDER

You have her father's love, Demetrius:
Let me have Hermia's; do you marry him.                                  95

### EGEUS

Scornful Lysander, true, he hath my love;

7

62 *estate* – "give" (as one leaves an estate to one's heir).
63 *as well derived* – "descended from as good a family".
64 *As well possessed* – "With as many possessions".
65 *as fairly ranked* – "considered as good".
66 *with vantage* – "with advantage", "better".
67 *prosecute* – "follow up".
68 *avouch . . . head* – "declare it in his face (straight before him)".
69 *Devoutly dotes, dotes in idolatry* – "Loves almost religiously, as if worshipping a god (*in idolatry*)".

70 *spotted* – "morally stained".
71 *being over-full of self-affairs* – "having too many of my own affairs to think about".
72 *lose* – "forget".
73 *schooling* – "instruction".
74 *arm* – "prepare".
75 *extenuate* – "soften (a punishment)".
76 *what cheer* – "how goes it with you?"
77 *Against* – "In preparation for".
78 *nearly that concerns* – "that closely concerns".

8

And what is mine my love shall render him;
And she is mine, and all my right of her
I do estate[62] unto Demetrius.

LYSANDER

I am, my Lord, as well derived[63] as he,                    100
As well possessed;[64] my love is more than his;
My fortunes every way as fairly ranked,[65]
If not with vantage,[66] as Demetrius';
And, which is more than all these boasts can be,
I am beloved of beauteous Hermia.                           105
Why should not I then prosecute[67] my right?
Demetrius, I'll avouch it to his head,[68]
Made love to Nedar's daughter, Helena,
And won her soul: and she, sweet lady, dotes,
Devoutly dotes, dotes in idolatry,                          110
Upon[69] this spotted[70] and inconstant man.

THESEUS

I must confess that I have heard so much,
And with Demetrius thought to have spoke thereof:
But being over-full of self-affairs,[71]
My mind did lose[72] it. But Demetrius, come,              115
And come Egeus, you shall go with me;
I have some private schooling[73] for you both.
For you, fair Hermia, look you arm[74] yourself
To fit your fancies to your father's will;
Or else the law of Athens yields you up –                  120
Which by no means we may extenuate – [75]
To death, or to a vow of single life.
Come, my Hippolyta; what cheer,[76] my love?
Demetrius and Egeus, go along:
I must employ you in some business                          125
Against[77] our nuptial, and confer with you
Of something nearly that concerns[78] yourselves.

79 *desire,* (to know more).
80 *How now* – "What is the matter?"
81 *How chance . . . fast?* – "How does it happen (*chance*) that the rose-like colour in your cheeks is fading so soon?" The rose as an image of woman's beauty repeats the idea in Theseus's speech (lines 77–9).
82 *Belike for . . . my eyes* – "Very likely (*Belike*) because these 'roses' are in need of rain (the company of Lysander), though I could pour enough water over (*beteem*) them from the storm in my eyes (from my tears)".
83 *Ay me* (an exclamation of grief).
84 *The course . . . smooth* – "True love was never like a river which flowed over a smooth course (its way was always rough)".

85 *different in blood* – "(concerned with lovers) of different descent (one noble, the other common)".
86 *cross* – "hindrance", "block".
87 *too high . . . to low* – "too noble to be bound (*enthralled*) to one to common birth".
88 *misgraffèd . . . years* – "wrongly united (*misgraffed*) from the point of view of their age (*years*)". *Misgraffed*: wrongly grafted (q.v.).
89 *spite* – "annoyance".
90 *engaged* – "bound", "promised".
91 *friends* – "close relations".
92 *by another's eyes* – "according to someone else's likings".
93 *sympathy* – "agreement".

EGEUS

With duty and desire[79] we follow you.

[*Exeunt.* LYSANDER *and* HERMIA *remain*

LYSANDER

How now,[80] my love? why is your cheek so pale?
How chance the roses there do fade so fast?[81]                130

HERMIA

Belike for want of rain, which I could well
Beteem them from the tempest of my eyes.[82]

LYSANDER

Ay me;[83] for aught that I could ever read,
Could ever hear by tale or history,
The course of true love never did run smooth;[84]              135
But either it was different in blood[85] –

HERMIA

O cross![86] too high to be enthralled to low.[87]

LYSANDER

Or else misgraffèd, in respect of years.[88] –

HERMIA

O spite![89] too old to be engaged[90] to young.

LYSANDER

Or else it stood upon the choice of friends – [91]             140

HERMIA

O hell! to choose love by another's eyes.[92]

LYSANDER

Or, if there were a sympathy[93] in choice,

11

94 *collied* – "black as coal".

95 *in a spleen unfolds* – "in sudden passion lays open to view".

96 *The jaws . . . up* – "The flash of lightning is swallowed up in darkness"; in such a way war, death, or sickness puts an end to love.

97 *confusion* – "defeat".

98 *an edict in destiny* – "an order (*edict*) made by fate".

99 *teach . . . patience* – "teach ourselves to be patient in this time of testing (*trial*)".

100 *customary* – "usual".

101 *As due* – "As much belonging".

102 *followers* – "companions"

103 *persuasion* – "belief".

104 *remote seven leagues* – "seven leagues (about twenty miles) distant".

105 *respects* – "regards"; "looks upon".

106 *without* – "outside".

107 *To do . . . May* –"To perform the ceremonies (*do observance*) of a first morning of May". On the first of May it was an ancient custom for young people to walk out into the woods or fields and bring back branches of trees or flowers, which were carried round the village.

108 *Cupid's strongest bow*. Cupid was the ancient god of love. He was imagined as a mischievous boy with a bow and arrows. These invisible arrows, shot into the hearts of young people, made them suffer the pains of love.

109 *head* – "tip of the arrow".

12

War, death, or sickness did lay siege to it;
Making it momentary as a sound,
Swift as a shadow, short as any dream,                    145
Brief as the lightning in the collied[94] night,
That in a spleen unfolds[95] both heaven and earth,
And ere a man hath power to say, Behold!
The jaws of darkness do devour it up;[96]
So quick bright things come to confusion.[97]            150

HERMIA

If then true lovers have been ever crossed,
It stands as an edict in destiny.[98]
Then let us teach our trial patience,[99]
Because it is a customary[100] cross,
As due[101] to love as thoughts, and dreams, and sighs,    155
Wishes and tears, poor fancy's followers.[102]

LYSANDER

A good persuasion;[103] therefore hear me, Hermia:
I have a widow aunt, a dowager
Of great revenue, and she hath no child;
From Athens is her house remote seven leagues,[104]       160
And she respects me[105] as her only son.
There, gentle Hermia, may I marry thee;
And to that place the sharp Athenian law
Cannot pursue us. If thou lov'st me, then,
Steal forth thy father's house tomorrow night;            165
And in the wood, a league without[106] the town,
Where I did meet thee once with Helena
To do observance to a morn of May,[107]
There will I stay for thee.

HERMIA

                    My good Lysander,
I swear to thee by Cupid's strongest bow,[108]            170
By his best arrow with the golden head,[109]

13

110 *simplicity* – "innocence".

111 *Venus' doves*. Venus, goddess of love, was Cupid's mother. Doves, of all birds the most faithful in love, were sacred to her.

112 *knitteth souls* – "ties souls together".

113 *that fire which burned . . . seen* – Dido was the Queen of Carthage. Her lover Aeneas (*the false Troyan*) had escaped from Troy. When he left her and sailed away to conquer Italy, in her grief she lit a great fire on the coast and threw herself into the flames. *Under sail* – "sailing away".

114 *appointed me* – "made an appointment with me".

115 *God speed* – "God bless you".

116 *whither away?* – "where are you going?"

117 *that fair again unsay* – "take back the word 'fair' which you have said about me".

118 *your fair* – "*your* fairness (beauty)".

119 *Your eyes are lode-stars* – "Your eyes are the ones that Demetrius follows". *Lodestars*: the stars that a ship steers by; hence, eyes that guide the lover.

120 *air* – "song".

121 *tuneable* – "tuneful".

122 *Sickness is catching . . . so*. We "catch" a sickness from another person; if one could "catch" a face (*favour*), Helena would like to have Hermia's.

123 *Demetrius being bated* – "Demetrius being left out"; "except for Demetrius"

124 *to you translated* – "changed into you". Quince uses the word of Bottom, III.i.99. Act II, sc. ii will show how mistaken is Helena in thinking this.

125 *sway the motion . . . heart* – "control the movement of Demetrius's heart"; i.e. decide whether it is to beat fast or slow in love – rule over his feelings: or perhaps, "decide in which direction his love will go".

126 *O that your frowns . . . skill* – "I wish my smiles could learn such skill (in making him love me) as your frowns have (in making him love you)".

By the simplicity[110] of Venus' doves,[111]
By that which knitteth souls[112] and prospers loves,
And by that fire which burned the Carthage Queen
When the false Troyan under sail was seen,[113]                    175
By all the vows that ever men have broke,
In number more than ever women spoke,
In that same place thou hast appointed me,[114]
Tomorrow truly will I meet with thee.

LYSANDER

Keep promise, love. Look, here comes Helena.                      180

*Enter* HELENA

HERMIA

God speed,[115] fair Helena, whither away?[116]

HELENA

Call you me fair? That fair again unsay.[117]
Demetrius loves your fair.[118] O happy fair!
Your eyes are lode-stars,[119] and your tongue's sweet air[120]
More tuneable[121] than lark to shepherd's ear,                   185
When wheat is green, when hawthorn buds appear.
Sickness is catching; O, were favour so,[122]
Yours would I catch, fair Hermia, ere I go.
My ear should catch your voice, my eye your eye,
My tongue should catch your tongue's sweet melody.               190
Were the world mine, Demetrius being bated,[123]
The rest I 'll give to be to you translated.[124]
O teach me how you look and with what art
You sway the motion of Demetrius' heart![125]

HERMIA

I frown upon him, yet he loves me still.                         195

HELENA

O that your frowns would teach my smiles such skill![126]

15

127 *His folly . . . of mine* – "I am not to blame for his foolishness (in hating you)".

128 *None . . . were mine* – "Only your beauty (is to blame); and I wish I had that beauty".

129 *he* – "my love" (line above).

130 *Phoebe.* Greek goddess of the moon, also called Diana.

131 *in the watery glass* – "in the still water that reflects the moon like a mirror (*glass*)".

132 *Decking . . . bladed grass* – "Ornamenting the blades (q.v.) of grass as if pearl, dissolved into liquid, had been poured over them".

133 *devised* – "planned".

*And therefore is winged Cupid painted blind* [146]

16

HERMIA

I give him curses, yet he gives me love.

HELENA

O that my prayers could such affection move!

HERMIA

The more I hate, the more he follows me.

HELENA

The more I love, the more he hateth me.                                    200

HERMIA

His folly, Helena, is no fault of mine.[127]

HELENA

None but your beauty; would that fault were mine![128]

HERMIA

Take comfort: he no more shall see my face;
Lysander and myself will fly this place.
Before the time I did Lysander see,                                        205
Seemed Athens as a paradise to me.
O then, what graces in my love do dwell,
That he[129] hath turned a heaven unto a hell!

LYSANDER

Helen, to you our minds we will unfold.
Tomorrow night, when Phoebe[130] doth behold                               210
Her silver visage in the watery glass,[131]
Decking with liquid pearl the bladed grass,[132]
A time that lovers' flights doth still conceal,
Through Athens' gates have we devised[133] to steal.

HERMIA

And in the wood, where often you and I                                     215

17

134 *faint* – "pale".

135 *Emptying . . . counsel sweet* – "Speaking out to one another all the sweet secret thoughts (*counsel*) of our hearts".

136 *stranger companies* – "strange companions".

137 *Keep word* – "Keep your promise".

138 *starve our sight From lovers' food* – "not let our eyes 'feed' upon the sight of one another (*lovers' food*)"; "not see each other".

139 *morrow deep midnight* – "to-morrow, as late as midnight".

140 *As you . . . on you* – "As much as you dote on Demetrius, may he dote on you".

141 *How happy . . . can be* – "How happy some people (such as Lysander) can be about others (such as Hermia)".

142 *his qualities,* i.e. the things which make up his character.

143 *holding no quantity* – "having no importance".

144 *transpose to form and dignity* – "change into things which have a proper shape and are deserving of respect". (Helena's words prepare us for the strange events in III.i).

145 *Love looks . . . mind* – "People in love see what they imagine (*with the mind*), not the reality which their eyes show them (*with the eyes*)".

146 *wing'd Cupid painted blind.* Pictures of Cupid often showed him with wings and a bandage over his eyes, representing love's "blindness".

147 *of any judgement taste* – "the least ability to judge (who should love whom)".

148 *Wings – unheedy haste* – "(The fact that Cupid has) wings but no power to see is a sign of (*figure*) haste without heed (*unheedy haste*)".

149 *waggish* – "mischievous".

150 *eyne* – "eyes".

151 *hail'd down oaths* – "poured down his oaths as forcefully and plentifully as if each oath was a hailstone".

152 *some heat from Hermia* – "some passion stirred up by Hermia's presence".

Upon faint[134] primrose-beds were wont to lie,
Emptying our bosoms of their counsel sweet,[135]
There, my Lysander and myself shall meet,
And thence from Athens turn away our eyes
To seek new friends and stranger companies.[136]      220
Farewell, sweet playfellow; pray thou for us;
And good luck grant thee thy Demetrius.
Keep word,[137] Lysander; we must starve our sight
From lovers' food,[138] till morrow deep midnight.[139]

LYSANDER

I will, my Hermia. [*Exit* HERMIA] Helena, adieu.      225
As you on him, Demetrius dote on you![140]

[*Exit* LYSANDER

HELENA

How happy some o'er other some can be![141]
Through Athens I am thought as fair as she.
But what of that? Demetrius thinks not so;
He will not know what all but he do know:      230
And as he errs, doting on Hermia's eyes,
So I, admiring of his qualities.[142]
Things base and vile, holding no quantity,[143]
Love can transpose to form and dignity.[144]
Love looks not with the eyes, but with the mind,[145]      235
And therefore is winged Cupid painted blind.[146]
Nor hath Love's mind of any judgement taste;[147]
Wings, and no eyes, figure unheedy haste;[148]
And therefore is Love said to be a child,
Because in choice he is so oft beguiled.      240
As waggish[149] boys in game themselves forswear;
So the boy Love is perjured everywhere;
For ere Demetrius looked on Hermia's eyne,[150]
He hailed down oaths[151] that he was only mine;
And when this hail some heat from Hermia[152] felt,      245

19

153 *he* – "the hail" (i.e. the oaths).
154 *showers of oaths did melt* – "all the oaths (compared to hail) melted away in this passion for Hermia (like hail-stones in sunshine)".
155 *intelligence* – "information".

156 *it is a dear expense* – "I shall have given a lot and got very little" (since Demetrius's thanks to Helena will only be for news of her rival).
157 *to enrich my pain* – "to increase my pain (of love)".

(I.ii) A group of working men meet to rehearse the play they wish to act before Theseus and Hippolyta in honour of the wedding. It will tell the story of the unfortunate lovers Pyramus and Thisbe. The parts are chosen, and they agree to meet at night in the wood.

1 *Quince . . . the tailor*. All these names are specially chosen to suggest the different trades. *Quince*: blocks of wood; *Snug*: tight fitting (as woodwork should be); *Bottom*: the base a weaver's thread is wound upon; *Flute*: the stop of an organ (which was kept in repair by the bellows-mender); *Snout*: nose of a kettle (mended by tinkers); *Starveling*: thin, starved-looking man (tailors were supposed to be thin). *Flute* also suggests a high voice like a flute: (he will act the part of Thisbe in their play).
2 *You were best* – "You would do best".

3 *generally*. Bottom often uses the wrong word; he means the opposite, "particularly" or "individually".
4 *scrip* – probably means "script": the paper with the play written on it. ("Scrip" had another meaning, as the little bag travellers used to carry).
5 *treats on* – "deals with"; "is about".
6 *actors* – "characters in the play".
7 *grow to a point* – "come to the point"; "start on the main business".
8 *Marry* – "Indeed" (from the oath "By Mary").

20

So he[153] dissolved, and showers of oaths did melt.[154]
I will go tell him of fair Hermia's flight;
Then to the wood will he tomorrow night
Pursue her; and for this intelligence,[155]
If I have thanks, it is a dear expense.[156]                    250
But herein mean I to enrich my pain,[157]
To have his sight thither, and back again.

                                                    [*Exit*


### Scene II. Athens.

*Enter* QUINCE *the carpenter*, SNUG *the joiner*, BOTTOM *the weaver*, FLUTE *the bellows-mender*, SNOUT *the tinker, and* STARVELING *the tailor*.[1]

#### QUINCE

Is all our company here?

#### BOTTOM

You were best[2] to call them generally,[3] man by man, according to the scrip.[4]

#### QUINCE

Here is the scroll of every man's name, which is thought fit, through all Athens, to play in our interlude before the Duke   5
and the Duchess on his wedding-day at night.

#### BOTTOM

First, good Peter Quince, say what the play treats on:[5] then read the names of the actors:[6] and so grow to a point.[7]

#### QUINCE

Marry,[8] our play is: 'The most lamentable comedy and most cruel death of Pyramus and Thisby'.                        10

21

9 *Masters,* **spread yourselves** – "Gentlemen, stand further back".

10 *ask* – "call for"; "need".

11 *look to their eyes* – "take care of their eyes" (there will be so many tears).

12 *move storms* – "stir up storms" (of tears).

13 *condole . . . measure* – "express considerable grief".

14 *humour* – "desire".

15 *Ercles.* Hercules: the strongest of all men in the ancient stories. A frequent character in the "interludes".

16 *rarely* – "finely".

17 *a part to tear a cat in,* i.e. a part that can be acted with much noise and fury.

18 **split,** with grief (though more probably, with laughter).

Lines 24–31: These verses are Bottom's idea of a fine tragic speech. Their style makes fun of the older kind of play.

19 *Phoebus' car.* Phoebus, god of the sun, was believed to ride across the sky each day in a great shining chariot (*car*).

20 *vein* – "style"; "way of speaking".

21 *condoling* – "gentle and sad".

*a part to tear a cat in,*[17] *to make all split* [18]

**BOTTOM**

A very good piece of work, I assure you, and a merry. Now, good Peter Quince, call forth your actors by the scroll. Masters, spread yourselves.⁹

**QUINCE**

Answer as I call you. Nick Bottom, the weaver.

**BOTTOM**

Ready; name what part I am for, and proceed.                    15

**QUINCE**

You, Nick Bottom, are set down for Pyramus.

**BOTTOM**

What is Pyramus, a lover or a tyrant?

**QUINCE**

A lover, that kills himself most gallant for love.

**BOTTOM**

That will ask¹⁰ some tears in the true performing of it. If I do it,
let the audience look to their eyes:¹¹ I will move storms;¹² I will    20
condole in some measure.¹³ To the rest – yet my chief humour¹⁴
is for a tyrant. I could play Ercles¹⁵ rarely,¹⁶ or a part to tear a
cat in,¹⁷ to make all split¹⁸:
The raging rocks
And shivering shocks                                                 25
Shall break the locks
Of prison-gates;
And Phoebus'¹⁹ car
Shall shine from far,
And make and mar                                                    30
The foolish Fates.
This was lofty! Now name the rest of the players. This is Ercles'
vein,²⁰ a tyrant's vein: a lover is more condoling.²¹

23

22 *take Thisby on you* – "take the part of Thisbe".

23 *a wandering knight.* In the middle ages, many stories were told of the adventures of knights (q.v.) who rode about the country doing brave deeds.

24 *Nay, faith* – "No, indeed".

25 *a beard coming* – (Flute's part was probably played by a boy actor).

26 *That 's all one* – "It makes no difference".

27 *small* – "low".

28 *An* – "If" (also in line 60).

29 *Thisne* – Bottom's way of pronouncing "Thisby" in "a monstrous little voice". In this play all the actors say "Thisby", but "Thisbe" is more correct.

24

QUINCE

Francis Flute, the bellows-mender.

FLUTE

Here, Peter Quince                                                                                  35

QUINCE

Flute, you must take Thisby on you.[22]

FLUTE

What is Thisby, a wandering knight?[23]

QUINCE

It is the lady that Pyramus must love.

FLUTE

Nay, faith,[24] let not me play a woman; I have a beard coming.[25]

QUINCE

That's all one;[26] you shall play it in a mask, and you may speak   40
as small[27] as you will.

BOTTOM

An[28] I may hide my face, let me play Thisby too: I'll speak in
a monstrous little voice: 'Thisne, Thisne'.[29] 'Ah Pyramus, my
lover dear! thy Thisby dear, and lady dear!'

QUINCE

No, no, you must play Pyramus; and Flute, you Thisby.            45

BOTTOM

Well proceed.

QUINCE

Robin Starveling, the tailor.

STARVELING

Here, Peter Quince.

25

30 *slow of study* – "taking a long time to learn (my part)".
31 *An . . . terribly* – "If . . . in a way that will cause fear".
32 *fright* – "frighten".
33 *every mother's son* – "every one of us".
34 *I grant you* – "I admit to you".
35 *aggravate* – "increase" (he means "reduce").
36 *sucking dove* – "infant dove" (which does *not* "suck").
37 *an 't were* – "as if it were". (an = "if".)

26

QUINCE

Robin Starveling, you must play Thisby's mother. Tom Snout, the tinker.                                                          50

SNOUT

Here, Peter Quince.

QUINCE

You, Pyramus' father; myself, Thisby's father; Snug the joiner, you, the lion's part: and I hope, here is a play fitted.

SNUG

Have you the lion's part written? Pray you, if it be, give it me, for I am slow of study.[30]                                    55

QUINCE

You may do it extempore, for it is nothing but roaring.

BOTTOM

Let me play the lion too; I will roar that I will do any man's heart good to hear me. I will roar, that I will make the Duke say, 'Let him roar again, let him roar again.'

QUINCE

An you should do it too terribly,[31] you would fright[32] the           60
Duchess and the ladies, that they would shriek; and that were enough to hang us all.

ALL

That would hang us, every mother's son.[33]

BOTTOM

I grant you,[34] friends, if you should fright the ladies out of their wits, they would have no more discretion but to hang us; but I     65
will aggravate[35] my voice so, that I will roar you as gently as any sucking dove;[36] I will roar you an 't were[37] any nightingale.

27

38 *a proper man . . . summer's day* – "as fine (*proper*) a man as one could see at the best of times (*a summer's day*)".

39 *you must needs* – "it is necessary for you to".

40 *discharge* – "perform".

41 *orange-tawny* – "dark orange-coloured". The colours Bottom mentions were fashionable for clothes not beards; as a weaver, Bottom's thoughts are chiefly about cloth.

42 *purple-in-grain* – "purple or scarlet, deeply dyed".

43 *French crown coloured* – "of the colour of the 'crown', or gold coin from France"; i.e. golden.

44 *crowns* – "crowns" meaning "heads".

45 *a mile . . . town.* This will be the place where Lysander is to meet Hermia (I.i.166). Shakespeare seems to have forgotten that it was a league, not a mile away.

46 *dogged* – "followed about" (as a dog follows people).

47 *a bill of properties*, a list of articles (*properties*) needed for the play.

48 *obscenely*, another mistake: *obscenely* = immorally; Bottom probably means "seemly" = "suitably".

49 *hold or cut bow-strings*, an old saying, meaning something like "keep on or give up entirely".

QUINCE

You can play no part but Pyramus; for Pyramus is a sweet-faced man, a proper man as one shall see in a summer's day,[38] a   70
most lovely, gentleman-like man; therefore you must needs[39]
play Pyramus.

BOTTOM

Well, I will undertake it. What beard were I best to play it in?

QUINCE

Why, what you will.

BOTTOM

I will discharge[40] it, in either your straw-colour beard, your   75
orange-tawny[41] beard, your purple-in-grain[42] beard, or your
French-crown-coloured[43] beard, your perfect yellow.

QUINCE

Some of your French crowns[44] have no hair at all, and then you
will play bare-faced. But, masters, here are your parts, and I am
to entreat you, request you, and desire you, to con them by   80
tomorrow night; and meet me in the palace wood, a mile
without the town,[45] by moonlight. There will we rehearse: for
if we meet in the city, we shall be dogged[46] with company, and
our devices known. In the mean time I will draw a bill of properties,[47] such as our play wants. I pray you, fail me not   85

BOTTOM

We will meet, and there we may rehearse most obscenely[48] and
courageously. Take pains; be perfect; adieu.

QUINCE

At the Duke's oak we meet.

BOTTOM

Enough; hold or cut bow-strings.[49]

*[Exeunt*

29

(II.i) Puck, a spirit of mischief, meets a fairy in the wood. They speak of
the quarrel between Oberon and Titania, king and queen of the fairies.
Oberon and Titania enter, and carry on their quarrel concerning the little
boy whom both claim as a follower. Because of this quarrel, the weather
has been upset and the crops have failed. When Titania leaves, Oberon
sends Puck for a magic flower. Its juice, put on the eyes of a sleeping person,
will make that person fall in love with the first live creature that is seen.
Oberon plans to bewitch Titania in this way.

Demetrius enters, pursued by Helena. Oberon overhears their conversation, and when Puck returns, orders him to use some of the juice upon
Demetrius so that he will love Helena as she loves him.

1 *How now* – "What's the matter?"
2 *Thorough* – "Through".
3 *park . . . pale* – "open grassland . . .
enclosed land" (*pale:* fence,
enclosure).
4 *the moones sphere.* The ancient
scientists taught that the sun, moon
and planets moved round the
earth in separate, constantly turn-
ing spheres. *moones:* old form of
*moon's.* The "e" should be pronounced for the line to be spoken
smoothly.
5 *To dew . . . green* – "To put dew on
the fairy orbs in the grass (*green*)".
*Fairy orbs:* circles of grass differently coloured from the rest.
Country people believed that they
were caused by fairies dancing in a
ring.
6 *her pensioners.* Queen Elizabeth's
guards were called "gentlemen
pensioners". They were young
noblemen chosen for their tall-
ness, and wore special coats orna-
mented with gold and jewels. The
Fairy Queen's "gentlemen pensioners" are the tall, gold-coloured
and red-spotted cowslips (q.v.).

7 *favours* – presents from a great person, to be worn as a sign of favour.
8 *hang . . . ear,* i.e. place a drop of
dew in each flower (like a pearl
worn on the ear).
9 *Lob* – name for a clown (q.v.).
10 *anon* – "immediately".
11 *Take heed* – "Take heed that".
12 *passing fell and wrath* – "extremely
fierce (*fell*) and angry (*wrath*)".
13 *Knight . . . train* – "one of the
knights (q.v.) who are his attendants (*train*)".
14 *trace* – "make his way through".

# ACT TWO

*Scene I. A wood near Athens.*

*Enter a Fairy at one side, and* PUCK *at another.*

PUCK

How now,[1] spirit, whither wander you?

FAIRY

Over hill, over dale,
Thorough[2] bush, thorough brier,
Over park, over pale,[3]
Thorough flood, thorough fire;                    5
I do wander everywhere,
Swifter than the moones sphere;[4]
And I serve the Fairy Queen,
To dew her orbs upon the green.[5]
The cowslips tall her pensioners[6] be;            10
In their gold coats spots you see,
Those be rubies, fairy favours,[7]
In those freckles live their savours.
I must go seek some dew-drops here,
And hang a pearl in every cowslip's ear.[8]         15
Farewell, thou Lob[9] of spirits; I 'll be gone;
Our Queen and all her elves come here anon.[10]

PUCK

The King doth keep his revels here tonight;
Take heed[11] the Queen come not within his sight;
For Oberon is passing fell and wrath,[12]           20
Because that she as her attendant hath
A lovely boy stolen from an Indian King;
She never had so sweet a changeling.
And jealous Oberon would have the child
Knight of his train,[13] to trace[14] the forests wild;   25

31

15 *perforce* – "by force".

16 *spangled starlight sheen* – "In the brightness (*sheen*) of starlight shining like spangles in the sky". *Spangles* = small, glittering objects stitched on clothes as an ornament.

17 *square* – "quarrel".

18 *making* – "appearance" (a person's "look").

19 *shrewd . . . Robin Goodfellow* – "mischievous and wickedly inclined spirit called Robin Goodfellow" (another name for Puck, who is often addressed in this play as Robin).

20 *villagery* – "village".

21 *bootless* – "without benefit".

22 *make the drink . . . barm*, i.e. put a magic spell upon the mixture from which beer is made, so that bubbles (*barm*) do not form and the drink is spoilt.

23 *harm* – "troubles".

24 *Hobgoblin . . . Puck.* These, with Robin Goodfellow, were names in different parts of the country for the same spirit.

25 *aright* – "rightly".

26 *in likeness of* – "in the shape of".

27 *gossip* – "country woman"; "neighbour in the village".

28 *crab* – "small apple". In winter these used to be roasted and dropped into a cup of beer to warm it.

29 *bum* – the sitting part of the body, the bottom.

30 *"tailor" cries* – an insulting word, not connected with "tailor" in the usual sense.

31 *falls into a cough* – "begins to cough".

32 *quire* – "company".

33 *And waxen . . . swear* – "And show increasing (*waxen*) mirth, and sneeze (*neeze*) and declare (*swear*)". (The sneeze was a sign that what had been said was true).

PUCK

32

But she perforce[15] withholds the lovéd boy,
Crowns him with flowers, and makes him all her joy.
And now they never meet in grove or green,
By fountain clear, or spangled starlight sheen,[16]
But they do square,[17] that all their elves for fear          30
Creep into acorn cups and hide them there.


FAIRY

Either I mistake your shape and making[18] quite,
Or else you are that shrewd and knavish sprite
Called Robin Goodfellow.[19] Are not you he,
That frights the maidens of the villagery,[20]          35
Skim milk, and sometimes labour in the quern,
And bootless[21] make the breathless housewife churn,
And sometimes make the drink to bear no barm,[22]
Mislead night-wanderers, laughing at their harm?[23]
Those that Hobgoblin[24] call you, and sweet Puck,[24]          40
You do their work, and they shall have good luck.
Are not you he?


PUCK
                    Thou speak'st aright;[25]
I am that merry wanderer of the night.
I jest to Oberon, and make him smile,
When I a fat and bean-fed horse beguile,          45
Neighing in likeness of[26] a filly foal;
And sometimes lurk I in gossip's[27] bowl,
In very likeness of a roasted crab;[28]
And when she drinks, against her lips I bob,
And on her withered dewlap pour the ale.          50
The wisest aunt, telling the saddest tale,
Sometime for three-foot stool mistaketh me;
Then slip I from her bum,[29] down topples she,
And "tailor" cries,[30] and falls into a cough;[31]
And then the whole quire[32] hold their hips, and laugh,          55
And waxen in their mirth, and neeze, and swear[33]

33

34 *room* – "make way".
35 *would that* – "I wish that".
36 *Ill met* – "A bad time for meeting".
37 *Tarry* – "Stay"; "Wait".
38 *Corin* – common name of a shepherd in ancient poems and stories.
39 *pipes of corn* – "musical pipes made of straw" (played by shepherds).
40 *versing love* – "composing love poetry".
41 *Phillida*. Phyllis; name given to the village girl beloved of Corin.

42 *steep* – "steep slope" or "cliff".
43 *forsooth* – "in truth"; "indeed".
44 *bouncing Amazon.* Amazons, according to ancient stories, were a tribe of fierce women fighters in South Russia; Hippolyta was their queen. *bouncing:* vigorous.
45 *buskined* – "wearing high boots" (for riding).
46 *glance at my credit* – "try to harm my good reputation (*credit*)".

*Your buskined[45] mistress*

34

A merrier hour was never wasted there.
But room,[34] fairy! here comes Oberon.

FAIRY

And here my mistress! Would that[35] he were gone!

*Enter* OBERON *the King of Fairies at one side with his train, and*
TITANIA *the Queen at another with hers.*

OBERON

Ill met[36] by moonlight, proud Titania.                                    60

TITANIA

What, jealous Oberon? Fairies, skip hence:
I have forsworn his bed and company.

OBERON

Tarry,[37] rash wanton; am not I thy lord?

TITANIA

Then I must be thy lady; but I know
When thou hast stolen away from fairy land,                               65
And in the shape of Corin[38] sat all day,
Playing on pipes of corn,[39] and versing love[40]
To amorous Phillida.[41] Why art thou here,
Come from the farthest steep[42] of India,
But that, forsooth,[43] the bouncing Amazon,[44]                           70
Your buskined[45] mistress, and your warrior love,
To Theseus must be wedded; and you come
To give their bed joy and prosperity.

OBERON

How canst thou thus, for shame, Titania,
Glance at my credit[46] with Hippolyta,                                    75
Knowing I know thy love to Theseus?
Didst thou not lead him through the glimmering night

47 *Peregenia ... Aegles ... Ariadne ... Antiopa,* names of women Theseus was said to have made love to in his many adventures. (The correct name of "Peregenia" was Perigouna).

48 *forgeries of jealousy* – "false stories made up by a jealous husband".

49 *the middle summer's spring* – "the beginning (*spring*) of full summer" (in England, early June).

50 *mead* – "meadow".

51 *pavéd fountain* – "fountain (q.v.) running over a natural floor of small stones".

52 *beachéd margent* – "sandy coast". (*margent* = margin, i.e. sea coast)

53 *ringlets* – "dances in a ring" (see note 5).

54 *piping to us in vain.* The idea is of the wind sounding like pipes for the fairies to dance to; but as the fairies no longer meet, it blows "in vain".

55 *Contagious fogs.* Thick mists (*fogs*) which were thought to spread illness (*contagious*).

56 *pelting* – "small and unimportant".

57 *proud* – (1) the usual meaning (as opposite to "pelting"); (2) "swollen" (with rain).

58 *overborne their continents* – "overflowed the banks which contain them (*their continents*)".

59 *stretched his yoke* – "pulled the plough to which he is tied". *yoke:* wooden piece laid over the necks of oxen while ploughing.

60 *lost his sweat,* i.e. wasted his hard work.

61 *ere ... beard* – "before it was old enough to grow a beard". The "head" of the corn, which must have grown before the corn is ready to be cut, is compared with the beard which must grow upon a boy before he can be considered a man.

62 *the crows ... murrion flock* – "the crows have fed until they are fat upon the bodies of the flock which have died of plague. *murrion* = murrain, q.v.

63 *the nine men's morris,* an old country game played with nine stones ("men") on each side, on squares cut in the ground with knives.

64 *And the quaint ... undistinguishable* – "And the complicated (*quaint*) winding paths (*mazes*) in the overgrown fields (*wanton green*) have not been trodden on for so long (owing to the rain) that they can no more be distinguished".

65 *want their winter cheer* – "lack (*want*) the food (*cheer*) which should be stored for winter".

66 *carol* – "cheerful song or dance" (modern "carols" are only sung at Christmas).

67 *the governess of floods* – "the power which controls (the tides of) the sea".

68 *washes ... air,* i.e. with rain.

69 *rheumatic diseases* – illnesses caused by dampness (coughs, colds, etc.).

70 *thorough this distemperature* – "through (because of) this disordered weather".

71 *hoary-headed* – "white-haired" (the frost is imagined as an old man with white hair).

72 *Hiems.* Latin name for winter, imagined as a man or spirit.

73. *An odorous ... set.* The buds of summer, standing out of the winter's ice, are imagined as a chain of flowers hung round the head of old Winter, as if to mock him.

74 *childing* – "fruitful"; "breeding".

From Peregenia,[47] whom he ravishéd?
And make him with fair Aegles break his faith,
With Ariadne, and Antiopa?                                    80

TITANIA

These are the forgeries of jealousy;[48]
And never since the middle summer's spring[49]
Met we on hill, in dale, forest, or mead,[50]
By pavéd fountain,[51] or by rushy brook,
Or in the beachéd margent[52] of the sea,                     85
To dance our ringlets[53] to the whistling wind,
But with thy brawls thou hast disturbed our sport.
Therefore the winds, piping to us in vain,[54]
As in revenge have sucked up from the sea
Contagious fogs;[55] which, falling in the land,             90
Have every pelting[56] river made so proud[57]
That they have overborne their continents.[58]
The ox hath therefore stretched his yoke[59] in vain,
The ploughman lost his sweat,[60] and the green corn
Hath rotted ere his youth attained a beard:[61]              95
The fold stands empty in the drownéd field,
And crows are fatted with the murrion flock;[62]
The nine men's morris[63] is filled up with mud,
And the quaint mazes in the wanton green,
For lack of tread, are undistinguishable.[64]                100
The human mortals want their winter cheer;[65]
No night is now with hymn or carol[66] blest;
Therefore the moon, the governess of floods,[67]
Pale in her anger, washes all the air,[68]
That rheumatic diseases[69] do abound.                       105
And thorough this distemperature[70] we see
The seasons alter; hoary-headed[71] frosts
Fall in the fresh lap of the crimson rose,
And on old Hiems'[72] thin and icy crown
An odorous chaplet of sweet summer buds                      110
Is, as in mockery, set.[73] The spring, the summer,
The childing[74] autumn, angry winter, change

75 *liveries* – as in I.i, 71.
76 *mazéd* – "confused".
77. *By their . . . which* – "Cannot tell one season from another by their products (*increase*)": summer has the ice of winter, winter the buds of summer.
78 *debate* – "dispute".
79 *We are . . . original* – "We have created these evils and are their origin".
80 *it lies in you* – "it is in your power".
81 *henchman,* boy attendant to a king on processions, marches, etc.
82 *the child of me* – "my child".
83 *spicéd* – "strongly scented".
84 *Neptune,* god of the sea.
85 *marking* – "looking at"; "taking notice of".
86 *traders* – "trading ships that have set out to sea (*embarkéd*)".

87 *the sails conceive . . . wind.* The ships' sails, swelled out by the wind, are thought of as if they were big with child.
88 *with pretty . . . gait* – "with a pretty way of walking like the movements of a swimmer".
89 *rich . . . squire* – "full of the child who is now my follower (*squire*)".
90 *would imitate . . . the land* – "would imitate by walking in a slow, stately way, like a ship sailing on land".
91 *mortal* – "human" (not a fairy, like Titania).
92 *of that boy did die* – "died in bearing that boy".
93 *stay* – "to stay".
94 *Perchance* – "Perhaps".
95 *in our round* – (in the fairy ring).

*the sails conceive,*
*And grow big-bellied with the wanton wind* [87]

38

Their wonted liveries,[75] and the mazéd[76] world,
By their increase, now knows not which is which.[77]
And this same progeny of evils comes                                    115
From our debate,[78] from our dissension;
We are their parents and original.[79]

OBERON

Do you amend it, then; it lies in you.[80]
Why should Titania cross her Oberon?
I do but beg a little changeling boy                                        120
To be my henchman.[81]

TITANIA

                                    Set your heart at rest;
The fairy land buys not the child of me.[82]
His mother was a votaress of my order,
And in the spicéd[83] Indian air, by night,
Full often hath she gossiped by my side;                                   125
And sat with me on Neptune's[84] yellow sands,
Marking[85] th' embarkéd traders[86] on the flood;
When we have laughed to see the sails conceive,
And grow big-bellied with the wanton wind;[87]
Which she with pretty and with swimming gait[88]                           130
Following, her womb then rich with my young squire,[89]
Would imitate, and sail upon the land[90]
To fetch me trifles; and return again,
As from a voyage, rich with merchandise.
But she, being mortal,[91] of that boy did die;[92]                        135
And for her sake do I rear up her boy,
And for her sake I will not part with him.

OBERON

How long within this wood intend you stay?[93]

TITANIA

Perchance[94] till after Theseus' wedding-day.
If you will patiently dance in our round,[95]                              140

39

96 *spare your haunts* – "keep away from where you are to be found".

97 *chide downright* – "quarrel openly".

98 *from* – "go from".

99 *injury* – "wrong (done to me)".

100 *Uttering . . . dulcet . . . . breath* – "Singing with such sweetness and harmony". *dulcet*: sweet.

101 *shot . . . spheres* – "rushed madly out of their spheres" (see note 4).

102 *a fair Vestal . . . west* – "a fair virgin ruling in the west" (i.e. Queen Elizabeth: see Introduction, p. xiv).

103 *love-shaft* – "arrow of love".

104 *As it should pierce* – "Strongly enough to pierce".

105 *might* – "could".

106 *Quenched . . . moon.* Cupid's arrow, which set hearts on fire with love, was stopped by the moonlight, like fire put out by water. (The moon as a goddess was thought to protect pure virgins who served her—"Vestals").

107 *imperial* – "royal".

108 *fancy-free* – "free from thoughts of love".

109 *bolt*, arrow.

*a mermaid on a dolphin's back*

And see our moonlight revels, go with us;
If not, shun me, and I will spare your haunts.[96]

OBERON

Give me that boy, and I will go with thee.

TITANIA

Not for thy fairy kingdom. Fairies, away:
We shall chide downright,[97] if I longer stay.                    145

[*Exit* TITANIA *with her train*

OBERON

Well, go thy way; thou shalt not from[98] this grove,
Till I torment thee for this injury.[99]
My gentle Puck, come hither. Thou rememb'rest
Since once I sat upon a promontory,
And heard a mermaid on a dolphin's back                         150
Uttering such dulcet and harmonious breath[100]
That the rude sea grew civil at her song,
And certain stars shot madly from their spheres[101]
To hear the sea-maid's music.

PUCK

I remember.

OBERON

That very time I saw, but thou couldst not,                     155
Flying between the cold moon and the earth,
Cupid, all armed; a certain aim he took
At a fair vestal thronéd by the west,[102]
And loosed his love-shaft[103] smartly from his bow
As it should pierce[104] a hundred thousand hearts;             160
But I might[105] see young Cupid's fiery shaft
Quenched in the chaste beams of the watery moon;[106]
And the imperial[107] votaress passed on,
In maiden meditation, fancy-free.[108]
Yet marked I where the bolt[109] of Cupid fell:                 165

C                                   41

110 *love-in-idleness*, a country name for the pansy, a small flower.

111 *or . . . or* – "either . . . or".

112 *I'll put . . . minutes* – "I will fly round the earth, as if tying a belt (*girdle*) on it, in forty minutes".

113 *the soul of love* – "the deepest love".

114 *render up her page* – "give up her boy attendant (*page*)".

115 *I am invisible*. This tells the audience that Oberon, though still on the stage, has made himself invisible to Demetrius and Helena.

116 *conference* – "conversation".

117 *The one . . . slayeth me* – "I will kill (*slay*) Lysander; Hermia is killing me (through my love of her)".

*a fair vestal thronèd by the west* [102]

42

It fell upon a little western flower;
Before, milk-white, now purple with love's wound,
And maidens call it Love-in-idleness.[110]
Fetch me that flower, the herb I shewed thee once.
The juice of it on sleeping eye-lids laid                    170
Will make or man or[111] woman madly dote
Upon the next live creature that it sees.
Fetch me this herb, and be thou here again
Ere the leviathan can swim a league.

PUCK

I'll put a girdle round about the earth                      175
In forty minutes.[112]

[*Exit* PUCK

OBERON

                  Having once this juice,
I'll watch Titania when she is asleep,
And drop the liquor of it in her eyes:
The next thing then she waking looks upon,
Be it on lion, bear, or wolf, or bull,                       180
On meddling monkey, or on busy ape,
She shall pursue it with the soul of love.[113]
And ere I take this charm from off her sight,
As I can take it with another herb,
I'll make her render up her page[114] to me.                 185
But who comes here? I am invisible,[115]
And I will overhear their conference.[116]

*Enter* DEMETRIUS, HELENA *following him*

DEMETRIUS

I love thee not, therefore pursue me not.
Where is Lysander, and fair Hermia?
The one I'll slay, the other slayeth me.[117]                190
Thou told'st me they were stolen unto this wood;

43

118 *wood* – "mad" (playing on "wood" in the usual sense).

119 *adamant* – "magnet" (a piece of metal so treated as to draw iron to it).

120 *true as steel*, a common expression for something quite faithful and dependable, like the steel of which swords are made.

121 *Leave you ... follow you* – "If you give up attracting me to you, I shall not be able to follow you".

122 *speak you fair* – "speak to you in a friendly, inviting way".

123 *Use me ... spaniel* – "Treat me as your humble dog".

124 *lose me* – probably means "loose me"; "turn me loose".

125 *give me leave* – "permit me".

126 *of high respect with me* – "which I would consider important".

127 *sick* – "sick in spirit", "miserable".

128 *impeach* – "expose to blame".

129 *commit* – "trust".

And here am I, and wood[118] within this wood,
Because I cannot meet my Hermia.
Hence, get thee gone, and follow me no more!

### HELENA

You draw me, you hard-hearted adamant,[119]                    195
But yet you draw not iron, for my heart
Is true as steel.[120] Leave you your power to draw,
And I shall have no power to follow you.[121]

### DEMETRIUS

Do I entice you? Do I speak you fair?[122]
Or rather do I not in plainest truth                           200
Tell you I do not nor I cannot love you?

### HELENA

And even for that do I love you the more.
I am your spaniel; and, Demetrius,
The more you beat me, I will fawn on you.
Use me but as your spaniel;[123] spurn me, strike me,          205
Neglect me, lose me;[124] only give me leave,[125]
Unworthy as I am, to follow you.
What worser place can I beg in your love,
And yet a place of high respect with me,[126]
Than to be uséd as you use your dog?                           210

### DEMETRIUS

Tempt not too much the hatred of my spirit;
For I am sick[127] when I do look on thee.

### HELENA

And I am sick when I look not on you.

### DEMETRIUS

You do impeach[128] your modesty too much,
To leave the city and commit[129] yourself                     215
Into the hands of one that loves you not;

45

130 *the opportunity of night* – "the opportunity provided by night".

131 *the ill . . . place* – "the evil thoughts that come to people in a lonely (*desert*) place".

132 *is my privilege* – "favours me".

133 *for that* – "because".

134 *It is not night . . . face.* Demetrius's face shines so brightly in Helena's eyes that there seems to be no night.

135 *worlds of company* – "al the company in the world".

136 *in my respect* – "to my way of thinking".

137 *the story shall be changed . . . chase.* Apollo, the beautiful sun god, was in love with a maiden called Daphne, and pursued her until she was magically changed into a tree. Now, says Helena, it is the man (*Apollo*) who flies, and the maiden who pursues (*holds the chase*).

138 *When cowardice . . . flies* – i.e., when the coward (*Helena*) pursues, and the brave one (*Demetrius*) flies.

139 *stay* – "stay for".

140 *Do not believe But* – "Do not believe anything else but that"; "be sure that".

141 *Ay, in the temple . . . mischief* – i.e. "you are wronging me in any place where I happen to be".

142 *set a scandal on my sex* – "bring all women (*my sex*) into disgrace".

*Apollo flies, and Daphne holds the chase* [137]

46

To trust the opportunity of night[130]
And the ill counsel of a desert place[131]
With the rich worth of your virginity.

HELENA

Your virtue is my privilege:[132] for that[133]                    220
It is not night when I do see your face,[134]
Therefore I think I am not in the night;
Nor doth this wood lack worlds of company,[135]
For you, in my respect,[136] are all the world.
Then how can it be said I am alone,                                225
When all the world is here to look on me?

DEMETRIUS

I 'll run from thee and hide me in the brakes,
And leave thee to the mercy of wild beasts.

HELENA

The wildest hath not such a heart as you.
Run when you will, the story shall be changed:                    230
Apollo flies, and Daphne holds the chase;[137]
The dove pursues the griffin, the mild hind
Makes speed to catch the tiger; bootless speed,
When cowardice pursues, and valour flies.[138]

DEMETRIUS

I will not stay[139] thy questions; let me go;                    235
Or, if thou follow me, do not believe
But[140] I shall do thee mischief in the wood.

HELENA

Ay, in the temple, in the town, the field
You do me mischief.[141] Fie, Demetrius;
Your wrongs do set a scandal on my sex:[142]                      240
We cannot fight for love, as men may do;
We should be wooed, and were not made to woo.

[*Exit* DEMETRIUS

47

143 *make a heaven of hell* – "find happiness in my worst misery".
144 *nodding* – "seeming to nod when the wind blows".
145 *over-canopied* – covered as if with a "roof" of flowers overhead. The Elizabethan beds had wooden roofs (*canopies*) over them; a bank with a canopy of flowers would suggest, to Shakespeare's audience, a fitting place for the Fairy Queen to sleep.
146 *luscious* – "thickly grown".
147 *the snake . . . enamelled skin* – snakes in England throw off their old skins every spring after the winter's sleep. *enamelled*: brightly coloured, as if painted.
148 *weed . . . fairy in* – "a garment (*weed*) wide enough for a fairy to wrap round itself" (the fairies being so little).
149 *this*, the magic flower Oberon holds in his hand.
150 *streak* – "rub gently over"; "stroke".
151 *hateful fantasies* – "love thoughts that would seem hateful to others".
152 *espies* – "sees".
153 *Effect* – "Perform".
154 *fond on* – "foolishly in love with"

*Quite over-canopied* [145]

48

I 'll follow thee, and make a heaven of hell,[143]
To die upon the hand I love so well.

[*Exit* HELENA

### OBERON

Fare thee well, nymph; ere he do leave this grove,                245
Thou shalt fly him, and he shall seek thy love.

*Re-enter* PUCK

Hast thou the flower there? Welcome, wanderer.

### PUCK

Ay, there it is.

### OBERON

                            I pray thee give it me.
I know a bank whereon the wild thyme blows;
Where oxlips and the nodding[144] violet grows,                250
Quite over-canopied[145] with luscious[146] woodbine,
With sweet musk-roses, and with eglantine;
There sleeps Titania sometime of the night,
Lulled in those flowers with dances and delight;
And there the snake throws her enamelled skin,[147]        255
Weed wide enough to wrap a fairy in;[148]
And with the juice of this[149] I 'll streak[150] her eyes,
And make her full of hateful fantasies.[151]
Take thou some of it, and seek through this grove:
A sweet Athenian lady is in love                                260
With a disdainful youth: anoint his eyes;
But do it when the next thing he espies[152]
May be the lady. Thou shalt know the man
By the Athenian garments he hath on.
Effect[153] it with some care, that he may prove          265
More fond on[154] her than she upon her love;
And look thou meet me ere the first cock crow.

### PUCK

Fear not, my lord; your servant shall do so.

[*Exeunt*

(II.ii) Titania is sung to sleep by her fairies on a bank covered with flowers. Oberon comes forward and puts the magic juice upon her eyes.

Lysander and Hermia enter. They are weary and lie down to sleep. Puck comes in, mistakes Lysander for Demetrius, and charms him with the juice.

Helena enters. Demetrius has escaped from her. As she stands there complaining, Lysander awakes, sees her, and falls in love with her. He follows her through the wood, leaving Hermia alone.

1 *roundel* – "round dance"; "dance in a ring".

2 *the third part of a minute* – "a third of a minute" – fairy time, like the forty minutes of Puck's flight (II.i.176).

3 *cankers,* insects in the early stage as worms, which eat rose-buds.

4 *war with* – "make war on".

5 *rere-mice* – "bats" (q.v.).

6 *quaint* – "pretty".

7 *offices* – "duties".

8 *with double tongue* – "forked"; "with two points".

9 *Philomel,* Greek name for the nightingale, a bird which sings by night.

10 *Lulla, lulla,* the beginning of *lullaby,* repeated to fit the tune of the song.

11 *spell* – "words of magic".

12 *our lovely lady nigh* – "near our lovely lady".

13 *spinners,* spiders (q.v.), which weave and spin webs.

14 *offence* – "harm".

15 *Philomel . . . etc.* The words from "Philomel" to "good night with lullaby" are repeated in the song as chorus.

*Scene II. The wood, with* TITANIA'S *sleeping-place behind.*

*Enter* TITANIA, *with her train.*

### TITANIA

Come now, a roundel,[1] and a fairy song;
Then, for the third part of a minute,[2] hence;
Some to kill cankers[3] in the musk-rose buds.
Some war with[4] rere-mice[5] for their leathern wings,
To make my small elves coats, and some keep back          5
The clamorous owl that nightly hoots and wonders
At our quaint[6] spirits. Sing me now asleep;
Then to your offices,[7] and let me rest.

*The fairies sing*

### FIRST FAIRY

*You spotted snakes with double tongue,[8]*
*Thorny hedgehogs, be not seen;*                          10
*Newts and blind-worms, do no wrong;*
*Come not near our Fairy Queen.*

### CHORUS

*Philomel[9] with melody*
*Sing in our sweet lullaby;*
*Lulla, lulla,[10] lullaby, lulla, lulla, lullaby.*       15
*Never harm, nor spell,[11] nor charm,*
*Come our lovely Lady nigh.[12]*
*So good night, with lullaby.*

### SECOND FAIRY

*Weaving spiders, come not here,*
*Hence, you long-legg'd spinners,[13] hence;*            20
*Beetles black, approach not near;*
*Worm nor snail do no offence.[14]*

### CHORUS

*Philomel with melody, etc.[15]*          [TITANIA *sleeps*

51

16 *aloof*-"apart from the others".
17 *Do it . . . take* – "Mistake it for your true love".
18 *ounce, cat,* wild cat.
19 *Pard* – "Leopard" (a dangerous wild animal with yellowish fur and dark spots).

20 *In thy eye* – "In your sight".
21 *faint* – "grow weary".
22 *tarry* – "wait".
23 *two bosoms and one troth* – "two hearts (bound by) one pledge of love (*troth*)".

### FIRST FAIRY

Hence away; now all is well;
One aloof [16] stand sentinel.                                    25

*[Exeunt Fairies*

*Enter* OBERON, *who puts the juice on* TITANIA'S *eyelids*

### OBERON

What thou seest when thou dost wake,
Do it for thy true love take: [17]
Love and languish for his sake.
Be it ounce, or cat, [18] or bear,
Pard, [19] or boar with bristled hair,                           30
In thy eye [20] that shall appear,
When thou wak'st, it is thy dear.
Wake when some vile thing is near.                          *[Exit*

*Enter* LYSANDER *and* HERMIA

### LYSANDER

Fair love, you faint [21] with wandering in the wood,
And to speak truth, I have forgot our way.                   35
We'll rest us, Hermia, if you think it good,
And tarry [22] for the comfort of the day.

### HERMIA

Be it so, Lysander; find you out a bed,
For I upon this bank will rest my head.

### LYSANDER

One turf shall serve as pillow for us both;                   40
One heart, one bed, two bosoms, and one troth. [23]

### HERMIA

Nay, good Lysander; for my sake, my dear,
Lie further off yet, do not lie so near.

53

24 *take the sense . . . innocence* – "understand (*take*) the true meaning (*sense*) of words that come from an innocent person".

25 *conference* – "speech"; "conversation".

26 *knit* – "bound together" (in common love).

27 *but one heart . . . it* – "we can only regard it (the hearts knit together) as one single heart".

28 *interchained* – "chained to one another".

29 *by your side no bed-room me deny* – "do not refuse (*deny*) me a place by your side where I may sleep (*bed-room*)".

30 *lying so . . . I do not lie.* Lysander plays on the two meanings of "lie". "I do not *lie* (tell lies) in saying I would lie so" (i.e. innocently).

31 *much beshrew* – "be much blamed".

32 *for* – "for the sake of".

33 *Becomes* – "Is fitting for".

34 *So far* – "As far as *this*" (Hermia points to the place where Lysander may lie down).

35 *end life* – "may my life end".

36 *With half . . . pressed* – "May your (the wisher's) eyes be closed together with half as much rest as you wish me (*half that wish*). (Lysander wished Hermia *all* sleep's rest. Hermia replies wishing him *half* of it – i.e. as much rest as hers).

37 *approve* – "try out".

38 *Weeds of Athens* – "Clothes in the Athenian style".

*Weeds of Athens*[38] *he doth wear*

54

#### LYSANDER

O take the sense, sweet, of my innocence.[24]
Love takes the meaning in love's conference.[25]          45
I mean that my heart unto yours is knit,[26]
So that but one heart we can make of it.[27]
Two bosoms interchainéd[28] with an oath,
So then, two bosoms, and a single troth.
Then by your side no bed-room me deny,[29]          50
For lying so, Hermia, I do not lie.[30]

#### HERMIA

Lysander riddles very prettily;
Now much beshrew[31] my manners and my pride,
If Hermia meant to say Lysander lied.
But, gentle friend, for[32] love and courtesy          55
Lie further off, in human modesty;
Such separation as may well be said
Becomes[33] a virtuous bachelor and a maid;
So far[34] be distant, and good night, sweet friend:
Thy love ne'er alter, till thy sweet life end!          60

#### LYSANDER

Amen, amen, to that fair prayer say I;
And then, end life,[35] when I end loyalty!
Here is my bed; sleep give thee all his rest.

#### HERMIA

With half that wish, the wisher's eyes be pressed![36]

*They sleep. Enter* PUCK.

#### PUCK

Through the forest have I gone,          65
But Athenian found I none
On whose eyes I might approve[37]
This flower's force in stirring love.
Night and silence: who is here?
Weeds of Athens[38] he doth wear:          70

39 *durst not* – "dares not".

40 *lack-love* – "person who lacks all feelings of love".

41 *kill-courtesy* – "person who would kill (put an end to) all courteous behaviour".

42 *Churl* – "Rough, bad-mannered man".

43 *owe* – "own".

44 *let love forbid . . . eyelid* – "may love forbid sleep to stay on your eyelid"; i.e. "may love keep you always awake".

45 *charge thee hence* – "command you to go from here".

46 *darkling* – "in the dark".

47 *on thy peril* – "at your own risk".

48 *fond* – "foolish".

49 *The more my prayer . . . grace* – "The more I pray (for Demetrius's love) the less favour (*grace*) does my prayer receive".

50 *came* – "became".

51 *washed*, i.e. with tears.

52 *ugly* – "frightening in appearance".

This is he, my master said,
Despiséd the Athenian maid:
And here the maiden, sleeping sound,
On the dank and dirty ground.
Pretty soul, she durst not[39] lie                    75
Near this lack-love,[40] this kill-courtesy.[41]
Churl,[42] upon thy eyes I throw
All the power this charm doth owe:[43]
When thou wak'st let love forbid
Sleep his seat[44] on thy eyelid.                     80
So awake when I am gone;
For I must now to Oberon.                   [*Exit*

*Enter* DEMETRIUS *and* HELENA, *running*

HELENA

Stay, though thou kill me, sweet Demetrius.

DEMETRIUS

I charge thee hence,[45] and do not haunt me thus.

HELENA

O wilt thou darkling[46] leave me? Do not so.         85

DEMETRIUS

Stay on thy peril;[47] I alone will go.

                                       [*Exit* DEMETRIUS

HELENA

O, I am out of breath, in this fond[48] chase,
The more my prayer, the lesser is my grace.[49]
Happy is Hermia, wheresoe'er she lies,
For she hath blesséd and attractive eyes.             90
How came[50] her eyes so bright? Not with salt tears:
If so, my eyes are oftener washed[51] than hers.
No, no, I am as ugly[52] as a bear;
For beasts that meet me run away for fear.
Therefore no marvel though Demetrius                  95

53 *Do as a monster* – "Run away as a wild beast (*monster*) would".

54 *glass* – "looking-glass"; "mirror".

55 *sphery eyne* – "eyes like stars in their spheres".

56 *Transparent*, plays on two meanings: (1) clear and beautiful; (2) able to be seen through – like glass. Meaning (2) leads on to the idea in the next line.

57 *That . . . thy heart* – "That lets me see your true feelings (*heart*) through their outer covering (*bosom*)".

58 *What though* – "What does it matter?"

59 *change . . . dove* – "exchange (*change*) a black bird of prey (*raven* – i.e. the dark Hermia) for a white and tame bird (*dove*, i.e. the fair Helena)".

60 *ripe not to reason* – "have not grown old (*ripe*) enough to act according to reason".

61 *touching . . . skill* – "coming now to the full knowledge of a man".

62 *marshal* – "directing force"; "guide".

63 *love's richest book*, Helena's eyes, full of loving looks (*Love's stories*) which Lysander believes he can "read".

Do as a monster,[53] fly my presence thus.
What wicked and dissembling glass[54] of mine
Made me compare with Hermia's sphery eyne?[55]
But who is here? Lysander on the ground!
Dead or asleep? I see no blood, no wound.                    100
Lysander, if you live, good sir, awake!

### LYSANDER (*awaking*)

And run through fire I will for thy sweet sake!
Transparent[56] Helena! Nature shows art,
That through thy bosom makes me see thy heart.[57]
Where is Demetrius? O how fit a word                         105
Is that vile name, to perish on my sword!

### HELENA

Do not say so, Lysander; say not so:
What though[58] he love your Hermia? Lord, what though?
Yet Hermia still loves you; then be content.

### LYSANDER

Content with Hermia? No, I do repent                         110
The tedious minutes I with her have spent.
Not Hermia but Helena I love:
Who will not change a raven for a dove?[59]
The will of man is by his reason swayed;
And reason says you are the worthier maid.                   115
Things growing are not ripe until their season;
So I, being young, till now ripe not to reason;[60]
And touching now the point of human skill,[61]
Reason becomes the marshal[62] to my will,
And leads me to your eyes, where I o'erlook                  120
Love's stories, written in love's richest book.[63]

### HELENA

Wherefore was I to this keen mockery born?
When at your hands did I deserve this scorn?
Is 't not enough, is 't not enough, young man,

59

04 *flout my insufficiency* – "mock at me for not being good enough" (to get a kind look from Demetrius).

65 *Good troth . . . good sooth* – "In truth" (*troth* and *sooth* have here the same meaning).

66 *me to woo* – "to woo me".

67 *perforce I must* – "I am compelled to".

68 *lord of* – "able to exercise".

69 *of* – "by".

70 *abused* – "deceived".

71 *mayst thou* – "may you be allowed to".

72 *leave* – "give up"; "no longer believe".

73 *my surfeit and my heresy.* He describes Hermia as a person he has loved too much (*surfeit*) and believed in mistakenly (*heresy*).

74 *powers* – i.e. powers of affection and strength.

75 *her knight,* to serve her faithfully, as knights served their ladies.

76 *Ay me, for pity!* – "Unfortunate me! have pity on me!"

77 *eat* – "ate".

78 *removed* – "gone away".

79 *Alack,* an exclamation of sorrow (like *alas*).

80 *and if* – "if indeed".

81 *of all loves* – "for the sake of all our love".

That I did never, no, nor never can                                    125
Deserve a sweet look from Demetrius' eye,
But you must flout my insufficiency?[64]
Good troth, you do me wrong, good sooth,[65] you do,
In such disdainful manner me to woo.[66]
But fare you well; perforce[67] I must confess                          130
I thought you lord of[68] more true gentleness.
O, that a lady of[69] one man refused
Should of another therefore be abused![70]                    [*Exit*

LYSANDER

She sees not Hermia. Hermia, sleep thou there;
And never mayst thou[71] come Lysander near.                           135
For, as a surfeit of the sweetest things
The deepest loathing to the stomach brings,
Or as the heresies that men do leave,[72]
Are hated most of those they did deceive;
So thou, my surfeit, and my heresy,[73]                                140
Of all be hated, but the most of me.
And, all my powers,[74] address your love and might
To honour Helen, and to be her knight![75]                    [*Exit*

HERMIA (*awaking*)

Help me, Lysander, help me! do thy best
To pluck this crawling serpent from my breast!                         145
Ay me, for pity![76] what a dream was here!
Lysander, look, how I do quake with fear.
Methought a serpent eat[77] my heart away,
And you sat smiling at his cruel prey.
Lysander! what, removed?[78] Lysander! lord!                           150
What, out of hearing? Gone? No sound, no word?
Alack,[79] where are you? Speak, and if[80] you hear:
Speak, of all loves;[81] I swoon almost with fear.
No? Then I will perceive you are not nigh.
Either death or you I 'll find immediately.

                                                               [*Exit*

                              61

(III.i) Bottom and his companions meet at the same place in the wood. They talk about their problems in acting the play. Puck overhears them rehearsing, and bewitches Bottom by placing an ass's head upon him. The others run away in fear; Bottom remains. At this moment Titania awakes, and falls in love with Bottom. She calls her fairies and orders them to attend him.

1 *Pat*– "Just in time".
2 *plot* – "piece of ground".
3 *tiring-house*, a room just behind the stage in Elizabethan theatres, where the actors changed their clothes. *tire* = attire; i.e. clothes. Quince has chosen the place where Titania is sleeping.
4 *in action*, not just speaking the words, but also acting the part.

5 *bully* – "friend"; "companion".
6 *cannot abide* – "cannot bear".
7 *By'r lakin*, a country oath, meaning "by our Lady".
8 *a parlous fear* – "a thing greatly to be feared". *parlous* = perilous, dangerous.
9 *not a whit* – "not in the least'.

# ACT THREE

*Scene I. The same place.*

TITANIA *sleeps. Enter* QUINCE, SNUG, BOTTOM, FLUTE,
SNOUT *and* STARVELING.

### BOTTOM

Are we all met?

### QUINCE

Pat,[1] pat; and here 's a marvellous convenient place for our
rehearsal. This green plot[2] shall be our stage, this hawthorn-
brake our tiring-house;[3] and we will do it in action,[4] as we will
do it before the Duke.                                                                       5

### BOTTOM

Peter Quince?

### QUINCE

What sayest thou, bully[5] Bottom?

### BOTTOM

There are things in this comedy of Pyramus and Thisby that
will never please. First, Pyramus must draw a sword to kill
himself; which the ladies cannot abide.[6] How answer you that?   10

### SNOUT

By 'r lakin,[7] a parlous fear.[8]

### STARVELING

I believe we must leave the killing out, when all is done.

### BOTTOM

Not a whit;[9] I have a device to make all well. Write me a

10 *for the more better assurance* – "to make them surer still".
11 *put . . . fear* – "take away their fear".
12 *in eight and six* – "in a line of eight syllables (q.v.) followed by one of six, then eight, and so on": a common kind of verse in the poems and songs of the time.
13 *two more . . . eight* – "two more syllables, making lines of eight syllables each". (But Snug's prologue in v.i is actually in ten-syllable lines).

14 *afeard* – "afraid".
15 *shield* – "protect".
16 *a more fearful wild fowl* – "a more frightening wild bird" (one of Bottom's usual mix-ups).
17 *look to 't* – "look into the matter".
18 *through . . . neck,* (in the skin the supposed "lion" will wear).
19 *defect* – meaning "effect" (*to the same effect* = "with the same meaning").
20 *it were pity of my life* – "I should be sorry to live".

prologue, and let the prologue seem to say, we will do no
harm with our swords, and that Pyramus is not killed indeed;   15
and for the more better assurance,[10] tell them that I Pyramus
am not Pyramus, but Bottom the weaver; this will put them
out of fear.[11]

QUINCE

Well, we will have such a prologue; and it shall be written in
eight and six.[12]   20

BOTTOM

No, make it two more; let it be written in eight and eight.[13]

SNOUT

Will not the ladies be afeard[14] of the lion?

STARVELING

I fear it, I promise you.

BOTTOM

Masters, you ought to consider with yourself, to bring in,
God shield[15] us, a lion among ladies is a most dreadful thing:   25
for there is not a more fearful wild fowl[16] than your lion
living; and we ought to look to 't.[17]

SNOUT

Therefore another prologue must tell he is not a lion.

BOTTOM

Nay, you must name his name, and half his face must be seen
through the lion's neck;[18] and he himself must speak through,   30
saying thus, or to the same defect:[19] "Ladies", or "Fair ladies",
"I would wish you" or "I would request you", or "I would
entreat you, not to fear, not to tremble: my life for yours. If
you think I come hither as a lion, it were pity of my life.[20]

21 *find out moonshine* – "find the
nights when the moon shines".
22 *disfigure* – meaning "figure" =
represent.

23 *present Wall* – "represent the
wall".

66

No, I am no such thing; I am a man as other men are"; and    35
there indeed let him name his name, and tell them plainly he is
Snug the joiner.

QUINCE

Well, it shall be so : but there is two hard things, that is, to bring
the moonlight into a chamber; for, you know, Pyramus and
Thisby meet by moonlight.    40

SNOUT

Doth the moon shine that night we play our play?

BOTTOM

A calendar, a calendar; look in the almanac; find out moonshine,[21] find out moonshine.

QUINCE

Yes, it doth shine that night.

BOTTOM

Why, then may you leave a casement of the great chamber    45
window, where we play, open, and the moon may shine in at
the casement.

QUINCE

Ay, or else one must come in with a bush of thorns and a lantern, and say he comes to disfigure,[22] or to present, the person
of moonshine. Then there is another thing; we must have a wall    50
in the great chamber; for Pyramus and Thisbe, says the story,
did talk through the chink of a wall.

SNOUT

You can never bring in a wall. What say you, Bottom?

BOTTOM

Some man or other must present Wall;[23] and let him have

24 *hold his fingers thus.* Bottom shows how with his own fingers.

25 *hempen home-spuns* – "coarse country people" (people wearing coarse cloth (see *hemp*) *spun* in their homes).

26 *cradle of the Fairy Queen*, the green bank where Titania lies asleep (see *cradle*).

27 *toward* – "about to take place".

28 *auditor*, listener to a play; one of the *audience*.

29 *An actor too.* Puck threatens to "act" as well as listen – by breaking into the rehearsal.

30 *odious* – "hateful": he means "odorous", i.e. sweet-smelling.

31 *hark* – "listen".

32 *by and by* – "very soon".

some plaster, or some loam, or some rough-cast about him, to  55
signify wall; or let him hold his fingers thus;[24] and through
that cranny shall Pyramus and Thisby whisper.

#### QUINCE

If that may be, then all is well. Come, sit down, every mother's
son, and rehearse your parts. Pyramus, you begin; when you
have spoken your speech, enter into that brake; and so every  60
one according to his cue.

*Enter* PUCK *behind*

#### PUCK

What hempen home-spuns[25] have we swaggering here,
So near the cradle of the Fairy Queen?[26]
What, a play toward?[27] I 'll be an auditor;[28]
An actor too,[29] perhaps, if I see cause.  65

#### QUINCE

Speak, Pyramus. Thisby, stand forth.

#### BOTTOM *as* PYRAMUS

Thisby, the flowers of odious[30] savours sweet.

#### QUINCE

Odours, odours.

#### BOTTOM *as* PYRAMUS

Odours savours sweet;
So hath thy breath, my dearest Thisby dear.
But hark,[31] a voice! stay thou but here a while,  70
And by and by[32] I will to thee appear.

[*Exit behind*

#### PUCK

A stranger Pyramus than e'er played here!

33 *marry* – "indeed".

34 *triumphant*. The word is meaningless here; so is "most lovely Jew" (line 79). Flute is putting in words to take the place of the ones he has forgotten.

35 *brisky juvenal* – "lively or quick-moving (*brisk*) young man (*juvenal*)".

36 *at Ninny's tomb*. Quince corrects this. "*Ninny*" = a fool.

37 *that . . . Pyramus*. The last line of "Thisby's" speech should not have been spoken until "Pyramus" replied.

38 *your cue is past* – "Your cue (q.v.) has already been spoken".

39 *pray, masters,* – "please, gentlemen".

40 *a round* – "in a circle".

**FLUTE**

Must I speak now?

**QUINCE**

Ay, marry,[33] must you; for you must understand, he goes but    75
to see a noise that he heard, and is to come again.

**FLUTE** *as* **THISBE**

Most radiant Pyramus, most lily-white of hue,
Of colour like the red rose on triumphant[34] brier,
Most brisky juvenal,[35] and eke most lovely Jew,
As truest horse, that yet would never tire.    80
I 'll meet thee, Pyramus, at Ninny's tomb.[36]

**QUINCE**

Ninus' tomb, man! Why, you must not speak that yet; that
you answer to Pyramus:[37] you speak all your part at once, cues
and all. Pyramus, enter: your cue is past;[38] it is "never tire".

**FLUTE** *as* **THISBE**

O, – As true as truest horse, that yet would never tire.    85

*Re-enter* BOTTOM *wearing an ass's head*

**BOTTOM** *as* **PYRAMUS**

If I were fair, Thisby, I were only thine.

**QUINCE**

O monstrous! O strange! We are haunted; pray, masters,[39]
fly! masters, help!

[*Exeunt all but* BOTTOM *and* PUCK

**PUCK** (*coming forward*)

I 'll follow you, I 'll lead you about a round,[40]
Through bog, through bush, through brake, through brier;    90

41 *And neigh . . . and roar*. Each noise
is typical of the animals mentioned in the next line (*neigh* for
horse, *bark* for hound, etc.).

42 *afeard* – see note 14.

43 *you see an ass-head of your own* –
"do you see your own head, looking like an ass's?" (Bottom has no
idea that he is wearing an ass's head
himself).

44 *translated* – "changed into another
being" (as in I.i.192).

45 *stir* – "move".

46 *ousel cock* – "blackbird"; the male
bird has shiny black feathers and a
bright yellow beak.

47 *throstle* – "thrush"; a brown singing bird with spotted breast.

48 *note so true* – "song (*note*) that is so
well in tune (*true*)".

Sometime a horse I 'll be, sometime a hound,
A hog, a headless bear, sometime a fire;
And neigh, and bark, and grunt, and roar,[41] and burn,
Like horse, hound, hog, bear, fire, at every turn.

[*Exit*

BOTTOM

Why do they run away? This is a knavery of them to make me     95
afeard.[42]

*Re-enter* SNOUT

SNOUT

O Bottom, thou art changed! What do I see on thee?

BOTTOM

What do you see? You see an ass-head of your own,[43] do you?

[*Exit* SNOUT

*Re-enter* QUINCE

QUINCE

Bless thee Bottom, bless thee! thou art translated![44]

[*Exit*

BOTTOM

I see their knavery: this is to make an ass of me, to fright me, if     100
they could; but I will not stir[45] from this place, do what they
can. I will walk up and down here, and I will sing, that they
shall hear I am not afraid. [*Sings.*

The ousel cock,[46] so black of hue,
With orange-tawny bill,                                            105
The throstle[47] with his note so true,[48]
The wren with little quill.

D                                    73

49 *The plain-song cuckoo*. The cuckoo
   bird is named after its unchanging
   cry of "cuckoo". *Plain-song* was
   the style of church music in the
   middle ages. It had not much
   variety; hence the cuckoo's song
   is here compared to it.

50 *answer "nay"* – "deny what the
   bird says" ("Cuckoo" being an
   insulting word for a married man
   – as if the bird were making fun of
   him).

51 *set his wit to* – "think out an
   answer to".

52 *give . . . the lie* – "tell the bird it is
   lying".

53 *he*, the bird.

54 *never so* – = "ever so"; "as much
   as it likes".

55 *mortal* – see note 91 to II.i.135.

56 *perforce* – "against my will".

57 *reason . . . together* – "reason and
   love have not much to do with
   one another".

58 *make them friends* – "bring reason
   and love together (in people's
   behaviour)". This is what happens by the end of the play (see
   Introduction).

59 *gleek upon occasion* – "make a
   clever remark (*gleek*) at the right
   time".

60 *to serve . . . turn* – "to attend to my
   own needs".

74

TITANIA (*awaking*)

What angel wakes me from my flowery bed?

BOTTOM (*sings*)

> The finch, the sparrow, and the lark,
> The plain-song cuckoo[49] grey;                    110
> Whose note full many a man doth mark,
> And dares not answer "nay".[50]

For indeed, who would set his wit to[51] so foolish a bird? Who
would give a bird the lie,[52] though he[53] cry "cuckoo" never
so?[54]                                                        115

TITANIA

I pray thee, gentle mortal,[55] sing again;
Mine ear is much enamoured of thy note;
So is mine eye enthralléd to thy shape;
And thy fair virtue's force perforce[56] doth move me
On the first view, to say, to swear I love thee.              120

BOTTOM

Methinks, mistress, you should have little reason for that: and
yet, to say the truth, reason and love keep little company together[57] nowadays. The more the pity that some honest neighbours will not make them friends.[58] Nay, I can gleek upon
occasion.[59]                                                  125

TITANIA

Thou art as wise as thou art beautiful.

BOTTOM

Not so, neither; but if I had wit enough to get out of this wood,
I have enough to serve mine own turn.[60]

TITANIA

Out of this wood do not desire to go;

75

61 *no common rate* – "no ordinary powers".
62 *The summer . . . state* – "All things that belong to summer serve me as their queen (*tend upon my state*)".
63 *the deep* – "the deep places of the sea".
64 *an airy spirit* – "a spirit made of air".
65 *Peaseblossom, etc.* – (see glossary). All the names suggest things that are small and light.

66 *hop in his walks* – "dance beside him where he walks".
67 *in his eyes* – "in his sight"; "where he can see you".
68 *apricocks* – "apricots" (q.v.).
69 *for night-tapers . . . thighs* – "take the wax from the top of the bees' legs to make candles for night" (*night-tapers*).
70 *To have . . . arise* – "to lead my lover to bed and back when he arises".

Thou shalt remain here, whether thou wilt or no.                    130
I am a spirit of no common rate;[61]
The summer still doth tend upon my state,[62]
And I do love thee; therefore, go with me.
I 'll give thee fairies to attend on thee;
And they shall fetch thee jewels from the deep,[63]              135
And sing, while thou on pressèd flowers dost sleep:
And I will purge thy mortal grossness so
That thou shalt like an airy spirit[64] go.
Peaseblossom, Cobweb, Moth, and Mustardseed![65]

*Enter Four Fairies*

FIRST FAIRY

Ready.

SECOND FAIRY

And I.

THIRD FAIRY

And I.

FOURTH FAIRY

And I.

ALL

Where shall we go?                    140

TITANIA

Be kind and courteous to this gentleman:
Hop in his walks,[66] and gambol in his eyes;[67]
Feed him with apricocks[68] and dewberries,
With purple grapes, green figs, and mulberries;
The honey-bags steal from the humble-bees,                    145
And for night-tapers crop their waxen thighs,[69]
And light them at the fiery glow-worm's eyes,
To have my love to bed, and to arise;[70]

77

71 *painted* – "brightly coloured".

72 *Nod* – "Bow your head".

73 *I cry . . . mercy heartily* – "I beg pardon (*cry mercy*) of you gentlemen (*your worships*) with all my heart". *Your worship:* a title of respect, *worship* meaning "a person of worth".

74 *I shall desire . . . acquaintance* – "I shall wish to be better acquainted with you".

75 *if I cut . . . you.* The countryman's way of healing a cut finger was to put a cobweb over the wound, which drew it together. *Make bold with:* "treat in a free or familiar way".

76 *commend me* – "speak well of me"; "give good wishes from me".

77 *Peascod* – "Pod"; the natural covering or shell in which peas grow.

And pluck the wings from painted[71] butterflies
To fan the moonbeams from his sleeping eyes;                150
Nod[72] to him, elves, and do him courtesies.

#### FIRST FAIRY

Hail, mortal!

#### SECOND FAIRY
   Hail!

#### THIRD FAIRY
    Hail!

#### FOURTH FAIRY
     Hail!

#### BOTTOM

I cry your worships mercy heartily;[73] I beseech your worship's
name?

#### FIRST FAIRY

Cobweb.                                                    155

#### BOTTOM

I shall desire you of more acquaintance,[74] good Master Cobweb: if I cut my finger, I shall make bold with you.[75] Your
name, honest gentleman?

#### SECOND FAIRY

Peaseblossom.

#### BOTTOM

I pray you, commend me[76] to Mistress Squash, your mother,   160
and to Master Peascod,[77] your father. Good Master Peaseblossom, I shall desire you of more acquaintance too. Your
name, I beseech you, sir?

78 *that same . . . house*, because mustard is put upon beef and eaten with it – so, says Bottom, the beef has "eaten up" Mustardseed's relations. *Of your house* – "of your family".

79 *made my eyes water*, not with tears of pity, as Bottom pretends, but because strong mustard makes the eyes water.

80 *wait upon him* – "attend him as servants".

81 *bower* – "inner room"; "bedroom". In the Elizabethan theatre, the "inner stage" would represent Titania's bower. She, Bottom and the fairies would go in and draw the curtains behind them. (See Introduction, p. xx).

82 *looks with a watery eye* – "shines through the clouds".

83 *Lamenting . . . chastity* – "Grieving at the virtue that is forced upon her" (spoken in pity of flowers that have not been able to bear seed; an idea well suited to a play in praise of marriage).

84 *Tie . . . tongue* – "do not let my lover speak".

(III.ii) Puck tells Oberon what has happened. Demetrius and Hermia enter. Hermia is angry with Demetrius: she blames him for Lysander's disappearance. She leaves Demetrius, who lies down to sleep.

Oberon sees that Puck has made a mistake. Puck is ordered to fetch Helena while Oberon charms Demetrius into loving her.

Lysander enters, begging Helena to love him. Demetrius wakes up, also in love with Helena. The two men quarrel, and Helena thinks they are both making fun of her.

Hermia comes in: nobody loves her now, and she blames her old friend Helena. There is a double quarrel, between the two girls and the two young men, which nearly ends in a fight. Oberon orders Puck to imitate the voices, now of Demetrius, now of Lysander, so that they fail to find one another in the dark. Finally, tired out with wandering, all four lovers come back one by one and fall asleep in the wood. Puck applies a remedy, so that when they awaken Lysander will love Hermia as before.

1 *came in her eye* – "came into her view".

2 *in extremity* – "to extremes".

3 *night-rule* – "entertainment of the night".

4 *close* – "secret".

5 *her dull and sleeping hour* – "the time when her mind is dull with sleep".

THIRD FAIRY

Mustardseed.

BOTTOM

Good Master Mustardseed, I know your patience well: that 165
same cowardly, giant-like ox-beef hath devoured many a
gentleman of your house.[78] I promise you, your kindred hath
made my eyes water[79] ere now. I desire you of more
acquaintance, good Master Mustardseed.

TITANIA

Come, wait upon him,[80] lead him to my bower.[81]           170
The moon, methinks, looks with a watery eye,[82]
And when she weeps, weeps every little flower,
Lamenting some enforcéd chastity.[83]
Tie up my love's tongue,[84] bring him silently.

[Exeunt behind

Scene II. Another part of the wood.

Enter OBERON

OBERON

I wonder if Titania be awaked;
Then, what it was that next came in her eye,[1]
Which she must dote on in extremity.[2]

Enter PUCK

Here comes my messenger. How now, mad spirit!
What night-rule[3] now about this haunted grove?          5

PUCK

My mistress with a monster is in love.
Near to her close[4] and consecrated bower,
While she was in her dull and sleeping hour,[5]

81

6 *A crew of patches* – "a group of clowns" (q.v.). *Patch* was often the word for a fool, who in Elizabethan comedies wore patched clothes.

7 *rude mechanicals* – "rough (*rude*) men who work with their hands".

8 *for bread* – "for a living".

9 *stalls* – "shops in the market".

10 *thick-skin . . . sort* – "person who lacks fine feelings (*thick-skin*), of that class of people (*sort*) which has no imagination".

11 *who Pyramus presented* – "who took the part of Pyramus".

12 *Forsook his scene* – "gave up (*forsook*) his part in the rehearsal".

13 *When . . . take* – "When I had this opportunity to deal with him".

14 *nole* – "head".

15 *Anon* – "At once".

16 *his Thisbe . . . answered* – "Thisbe's speech in the play needed an answer".

17 *forth my mimic comes* – "out comes my imitation (*mimic*) (of Pyramus's voice)".

18 *the creeping fowler eye* – "see the fowler (q.v.) creeping towards them".

19 *russet-pated choughs* – "crows (q.v.) with reddish-coloured (*russet*) heads (*pates*)".

20 *in sort* – "in company".

21 *Sever themselves* – "Separate themselves one from the other".

22 *sweep* – "fly across".

23 *at his sight* – "at the sight of Bottom".

24 *fellows* – "companions" (Bottom's friends fled in separate directions like birds frightened by a gunshot).

25 *our stamp* – "the sound of my (Puck's) feet as I stamped on the ground".

26 *Their sense thus weak* – "Their power of reason, as weak as I have described".

27 *senseless things* – "things without feelings", i.e. plants, bushes, etc.

28 *at their apparel snatch* – "pull at their clothes".

29 *from yielders all things catch* – "they (briers and thorns) catch everything from men who give everything away (*yielders*)".

30 *translated* – see note 44 to III.i.

31 *came to pass* – "happened".

32 *latched* – "made wet".

33 *of force . . . eyed* – "of necessity she must be seen by him".

A crew of patches,[6] rude mechanicals,[7]
That work for bread[8] upon Athenian stalls,[9]                    10
Were met together to rehearse a play
Intended for great Theseus' nuptial-day.
The shallowest thick-skin of that barren sort,[10]
Who Pyramus presented,[11] in their sport
Forsook his scene[12] and entered in a brake;                     15
When I did him at this advantage take,[13]
An ass's nole[14] I fixéd on his head.
Anon[15] his Thisbe must be answeréd,[16]
And forth my mimic comes.[17] When they him spy,
As wild geese that the creeping fowler eye,[18]                   20
Or russet-pated choughs,[19] many in sort,[20]
Rising and cawing at the gun's report,
Sever themselves[21] and madly sweep[22] the sky,
So at his sight,[23] away his fellows[24] fly;
And at our stamp[25] here, o'er and o'er one falls;               25
He "murder" cries, and help from Athens calls.
Their sense thus weak,[26] lost with their fears thus strong,
Made senseless things[27] begin to do them wrong;
For briers and thorns at their apparel snatch;[28]
Some sleeves, some hats; from yielders all things catch.[29]      30
I led them on in this distracted fear,
And left sweet Pyramus translated[30] there;
When in that moment, so it came to pass,[31]
Titania waked, and straightway loved an ass.

OBERON

This falls out better than I could devise.                        35
But hast thou yet latched[32] the Athenian's eyes
With the love-juice, as I did bid thee do?

PUCK

I took him sleeping – that is finished too –
And the Athenian woman by his side;
That, when he waked, of force she must be eyed.[33]               40

83

34 *close* – "hidden".

35 *not this the man* – (Puck expects to see Lysander, not Demetrius).

36 *Lay breath . . . foe* – "Speak so bitterly to a bitter foe (and not to me)".

37 *use* – "treat".

38 *Being o'er shoes . . . too* – "since you have already stepped into blood so that it covers your shoes (by killing Lysander) you may as well plunge deep into blood and kill me too". So Macbeth, after murdering Banquo, says: "I am in blood Stepped in so far that, should I wade no more, Returning were as tedious as go o'er". The image is of a river of blood that must be crossed.

39 *true* – "faithful".

40 *bored* – "have a hole pierced through it".

41 *the moon* – "the moon's light".

42 *displease . . . Antipodes* – "spoil the light at mid-day made by the sun, her brother, on the other side of the world (*Antipodes*)". Shakespeare is thinking of a flat earth, where the sun shines "underneath" during our night. Actually day and night are to east and west, not north and south of the globe.

43 *yonder Venus* – "the planet named Venus up there (in the sky)".

44 *in . . . sphere* – "sphere": see note 4 to II.i.

*Rising and cawing at the gun's report*
*Sever themselves*[21] *and madly sweep*[22] *the sky*

*Enter* DEMETRIUS *and* HERMIA

OBERON

Stand close:[34] this is the same Athenian.

PUCK

This is the woman, but not this the man.[35]

DEMETRIUS

O, why rebuke you him that loves you so?
Lay breath so bitter on your bitter foe.[36]

HERMIA

Now I but chide, but I should use[37] thee worse,       45
For thou, I fear, hast given me cause to curse.
If thou hast slain Lysander in his sleep,
Being o'er shoes in blood, plunge in the deep,
And kill me too.[38]
The sun was not so true[39] unto the day       50
As he to me. Would he have stolen away
From sleeping Hermia? I 'll believe as soon
This whole earth may be bored,[40] and that the moon[41]
May through the centre creep, and so displease
Her brother's noontide with the Antipodes.[42]       55
It cannot be but thou hast murdered him;
So should a murderer look; so dead, so grim.

DEMETRIUS

So should the murdered look; and so should I,
Pierced through the heart with your stern cruelty:
Yet you, the murderer, look as bright, as clear       60
As yonder Venus[43] in her glimmering sphere.[44]

HERMIA

What 's this to my Lysander? Where is he?
Ah, good Demetrius, wilt thou give him me?

45 *numbered* – "counted in"; "included".

46 *Durst thou* – "Would you have dared to".

47 *being awake* – "when he (Lysander) was awake".

48 *touch* – "action"; "deed".

49 *with doubler . . . stung* – "no snake ever stung more deceitfully". Hermia plays on (1) the "double" tongue of the snake (II.ii.9); (2) the "double tongue" of what she thinks is deceit (double meaning) in Demetrius's speeches.

50 *misprised mood* – "mistaken (*misprised*) set of ideas".

51 *aught* – "anything".

52 *tell* – "know'.

53 *An if* – "If".

54 *in . . . vein* – "while she speaks in this fierce way".

55 *For debt . . . owe* – "Because the amount of sleep which is due to ease my sorrow has not been paid". The idea is that sleep is owing to sorrow like a debt owed by a bankrupt; since sleep has not "paid up", the sorrow grows harder to bear.

DEMETRIUS

I had rather give his carcass to my hounds.

HERMIA

Out, dog! out, cur! thou drivest me past the bounds 65
Of maiden's patience. Hast thou slain him, then?
Henceforth be never numbered[45] among men!
O, once tell true; tell true, even for my sake:
Durst thou[46] have looked upon him, being awake?[47]
And hast thou killed him sleeping? O brave touch![48] 70
Could not a worm, an adder do so much?
An adder did it: for with doubler tongue
Than thine, thou serpent, never adder stung.[49]

DEMETRIUS

You spend your passion on a misprised mood:[50]
I am not guilty of Lysander's blood; 75
Nor is he dead, for aught[51] that I can tell.[52]

HERMIA

I pray thee tell me then that he is well.

DEMETRIUS

An if[53] I could, what should I get therefore?

HERMIA

A privilege, never to see me more.
And from thy hated presence part I so: 80
See me no more, whether he be dead or no.

[Exit

DEMETRIUS

There is no following her in this fierce vein;[54]
Here therefore for a while I will remain.
So sorrow's heaviness doth heavier grow
For debt that bankrupt sleep doth sorrow owe,[55] 85

87

56 *in some . . . stay* – "now sleep will pay a little of its debt, if I stay till it makes an offer (*tender*)", i.e. if I wait now, I can expect a little sleep to relieve my sorrow.

57 *true-love's* – "true lover's".

58 *Of thy misprision . . . ensue* – "There must of necessity result (*ensue*) from your mistake (*misprision*)".

59 *turned* – "changed into the opposite (into a false lover)". Puck's mistake, says Oberon, will mislead a true lover instead of correcting a false one.

60 *o'er-rules* – "decides".

61 *that one man . . . troth* – "that for one man who keeps his pledge".

62 *confounding . . . oath* – "making one promise contrary to another".

63 *fancy-sick* – "love-sick".

64 *cheer* – "face".

65 *With sighs . . . dear.* It was thought that sighing used up the air in the blood and caused paleness.

66 *illusion* – "trick".

67 *against . . . appear* – "in readiness for when she appears".

68 *the Tartar's bow.* The Tartars were a fierce fighting people in south Russia, famous for their skill with the bow and arrow.

69 *Sink* – "Strike deep".

70 *in apple of his eye* – "in the pupil (the circular opening in the centre) of his eye" – i.e. may the love magic deeply influence his sight.

*Swifter than arrow from the Tartar's bow* [68]

Which now in some slight measure it will pay,
If for his tender here I make some stay.[56]

*[Lies down and sleeps*

OBERON

What hast thou done? Thou hast mistaken quite,
And laid the love-juice on some true-love's[57] sight.
Of thy misprision must perforce ensue[58]                          90
Some true love turned,[59] and not a false turned true.

PUCK

Then fate o'er-rules,[60] that, one man holding troth,[61]
A million fail, confounding oath on oath.[62]

OBERON

About the wood go swifter than the wind,
And Helena of Athens look thou find.                               95
All fancy-sick[63] she is and pale of cheer[64]
With sighs of love that cost the fresh blood dear.[65]
By some illusion[66] see thou bring her here;
I 'll charm his eyes against she do appear.[67]

PUCK

I go, I go, look how I go,                                         100
Swifter than arrow from the Tartar's bow.[68]

*[Exit*

OBERON

Flower of this purple dye,
Hit with Cupid's archery,
Sink[69] in apple of his eye.[70]
When his love he doth espy,                                       105
Let her shine as gloriously
As the Venus of the sky.
When thou wak'st, if she be by,
Beg of her for remedy.

71 *the youth*, i.e. Lysander.
72 *a lover's fee* – "a lover's reward" (which is love in return).
73 *pageant* – "performance" (as of a play).
74 *sport alone* – "amusement in itself – without more added".
75 *befall preposterously* – "happen (*befall*) quite out of the natural order of things".
76 *come in* – "appear in".
77 *vows so born . . . appears* – "full truth will follow from vows that have their origin (*nativity*) in tears".
78 *Bearing . . . true* – "Since they bear the distinctive sign (*badge*) of my faith" (the "badge of faith" being his tears).

79 *advance* – "increase".
80 *When troth kills truth . . . fray* – "When one's spoken pledge (*troth*) destroys the truth, it is a struggle (*fray*) between what is devilish (false pledges) and what is holy (the truth)".
81 *Weigh oath . . . weigh* – "If you were to weigh (the importance of) your vow to Hermia against your vow to me, there would be no difference between them (*they would nothing weigh*)".

*Re-enter* PUCK

PUCK

Captain of our fairy band,                       110
Helena is here at hand,
And the youth,[71] mistook by me,
Pleading for a lover's fee.[72]
Shall we their fond pageant[73] see?
Lord, what fools these mortals be!               115

OBERON

Stand aside: the noise they make
Will cause Demetrius to awake.

PUCK

Then will two at once woo one;
That must needs be sport alone;[74]
And those things do best please me          120
That befall preposterously.[75]

                          [*They stand behind*

*Enter* LYSANDER *and* HELENA

LYSANDER

Why should you think that I should woo in scorn?
Scorn and derision never come in[76] tears:
Look, when I vow I weep; and vows so born
In their nativity all truth appears.[77]           125
How can these things in me seem scorn to you,
Bearing the badge of faith to prove them true?[78]

HELENA

You do advance[79] your cunning more and more.
When troth kills truth, O devilish-holy fray![80]
These vows are Hermia's: will you give her o'er?    130
Weigh oath with oath, and you will nothing weigh.[81]

82 *even* – "equal".
83 *as light as tales* – "as light in weight (unimportant) as stories with no truth in them".
84 *judgement* – "ability to reason".
85 *in my mind* – "in my opinion".
86 *high Taurus' snow* – "the snow on the high mountains of Taurus (in Turkey)".
87 *Fanned* with – "When blown upon".
88 *This Princess . . . white*, i.e. Helena's white hand.

89 *this seal of bliss* – "this which seals (completes) a perfect joy".
90 *bent* – "determined".
91 *set against* – "make an attack upon".
92 *civil* – "polite".
93 *in souls* – "in mind".
94 *in show* – "in outward appearance".
95 *superpraise my parts* – "over-praise my good qualities (*parts*)".
96 *trim* – "fine".

Your vows to her and me, put in two scales,
Will even[82] weigh; and both as light as tales.[83]

LYSANDER
I had no judgement[84] when to her I swore.

HELENA
Nor none, in my mind,[85] now you give her o'er.                    135

LYSANDER
Demetrius loves her, and he loves not you.

DEMETRIUS (*awaking*)
O Helen, goddess, nymph, perfect, divine,
To what, my love, shall I compare thine eyne?
Crystal is muddy: O how ripe in show
Thy lips, those kissing cherries, tempting grow!                    140
That pure congealéd white, high Taurus' snow,[86]
Fanned with[87] the eastern wind, turns to a crow
When thou hold'st up thy hand. O let me kiss
This princess of pure white,[88] this seal of bliss![89]

HELENA
O spite! O hell! I see you all are bent[90]                         145
To set against[91] me for your merriment:
If you were civil,[92] and knew courtesy,
You would not do me thus much injury.
Can you not hate me, as I know you do,
But you must join in souls[93] to mock me too?                      150
If you were men, as men you are in show,[94]
You would not use a gentle lady so;
To vow, and swear, and superpraise my parts,[95]
When I am sure you hate me with your hearts.
You both are rivals, and love Hermia;                               155
And now both rivals, to mock Helena.
A trim[96] exploit, a manly enterprise,

93

97 *conjure tears up* – "bring tears into being".

98 *sort* – "rank"; "class".

99 *extort* – "torture".

100 *part* – "share".

101 *more idle breath* – "more useless words".

102 *I will none* – "I want nothing of her".

103 *My heart . . . sojourned* – "My heart travelled (*sojourned*) to her only as a guest might (*guest-wise*)".

104 *Lest . . . dear* – "Lest you take the risk of paying dearly for it (*aby it dear*)".

105 *his function takes* – "takes away its (the eye's) power of seeing".

To conjure tears up[97] in a poor maid's eyes
With your derision! None of noble sort[98]
Would so offend a virgin, and extort[99]          160
A poor soul's patience, all to make you sport.

### LYSANDER

You are unkind, Demetrius; be not so;
For you love Hermia; this you know I know;
And here with all good will, with all my heart,
In Hermia's love I yield you up my part;[100]          165
And yours of Helena to me bequeath,
Whom I do love, and will do till my death.

### HELENA

Never did mockers waste more idle breath.[101]

### DEMETRIUS

Lysander, keep thy Hermia; I will none.[102]
If e'er I loved her, all that love is gone.          170
My heart to her but as guest-wise sojourned,[103]
And now to Helen is it home returned,
There to remain.

### LYSANDER

                    Helen, it is not so.

### DEMETRIUS

Disparage not the faith thou dost not know,
Lest to thy peril thou aby it dear.[104]          175
Look where thy love comes; yonder is thy dear.

*Enter* HERMIA

### HERMIA

Dark night, that from the eye his function takes,[105]

106 *The ear . . . makes* – "Makes the ear all the readier to understand".
107 *Wherein . . . recompense* – "While it impairs the sight, it gives the hearing a double reward (*recompense*)"; i.e. the less we see at night, the more we hear.
108 *thy sound* – "the sound of you".
109 *bide* – "stay".
110 *engilds* – "makes bright with golden light".
111 *oes and eyes of light* – "little circles and strokes (shaped like o and i) of light" – i.e. stars.

112 *bare* – "bore", "felt towards".
113 *confederacy* – "group of persons plotting together".
114 *conjoined* – "joined together".
115 *to fashion . . . me* – "to plan this cruel game in order to wrong me".
116 *Injurious* – "Wrong-doing".
117 *sisters' vows* – "vows to be like sisters to one another".
118 *chid . . . time* – "blamed (*chid*) the fast-moving (*hasty-footed*) time".

The ear more quick of apprehension makes;[106]
Wherein it doth impair the seeing sense,
It pays the hearing double recompense.[107]                    180
Thou art not by mine eye, Lysander, found;
Mine ear, I thank it, brought me to thy sound.[108]
But why unkindly didst thou leave me so?

LYSANDER

Why should he stay whom love doth press to go?

HERMIA

What love could press Lysander from my side?              185

LYSANDER

Lysander's love, that would not let him bide;[109]
Fair Helena, who more engilds[110] the night
Than all yon fiery oes and eyes of light.[111]
Why seek'st thou me? Could not this make thee know
The hate I bare[112] thee made me leave thee so?          190

HERMIA

You speak not as you think; it cannot be.

HELENA

Lo, she is one of this confederacy![113]
Now I perceive they have conjoined,[114] all three,
To fashion this false sport in spite of me.[115]
Injurious[116] Hermia, most ungrateful maid!              195
Have you conspired, have you with these contrived
To bait me with this foul derision?
Is all the counsel that we two have shared,
The sisters' vows,[117] the hours that we have spent,
When we have chid the hasty-footed time[118]              200
For parting us, – O, is all forgot?
All school-days' friendship, childhood innocence?

97

119 *artificial gods* – "gods at their work of creating".

120 *warbling* – "singing in a gentle, continuous tone" (like bird song).

121 *in one key* – "in one set of musical sounds".

122 *incorporate* – "forming one single body".

123 *double cherry* – "two cherries growing under a single skin".

124 *an union in partition* – "one person in spite of being divided (*in partition*)".

125 *Two of the first* – "Two bodies".

126 *like coats in heraldry . . . crest* – "like two coats of arms (q.v.) belonging to one nobleman, as appears from the one crest (q.v.) standing above them (*crowned*)".

127 *rent asunder* – "tear apart".

128 *Our sex, as well as I* – "All women, and not only I".

129 *set* – "set on"; "encouraged".

130 *so rich . . . soul* – "so precious in his thoughts".

131 *tender* – "offer".

132 *affection* – "passionate desire" (not true love).

133 *in grace* – "in favour".

134 *hung upon with love* – "followed about with loving behaviour"; or perhaps "covered all over with love" (like a tree with fruit).

135 *to love unloved* – "to love and not be loved in return".

*Two of the first,*[125] *like coats in heraldry,*
*Due but to one and crownéd with one crest* [126]

98

We, Hermia, like two artificial gods,[119]
Have with our needles created both one flower,
Both on one sampler, sitting on one cushion,                           205
Both warbling[120] of one song, both in one key;[121]
As if our hands, our sides, voices, and minds
Had been incorporate.[122] So we grew together,
Like to a double cherry,[123] seeming parted,
But yet an union in partition,[124]                                    210
Two lovely berries, moulded on one stem;
So, with two seeming bodies, but one heart;
Two of the first,[125] like coats in heraldry,
Due but to one and crownéd with one crest.[126]
And will you rent our ancient love asunder,[127]                       215
To join with men in scorning your poor friend?
It is not friendly, 't is not maidenly.
Our sex, as well as I,[128] may chide you for it,
Though I alone do feel the injury.

HERMIA

I am amazéd at your passionate words;                                  220
I scorn you not; it seems that you scorn me.

HELENA

Have you not set[129] Lysander, as in scorn,
To follow me, and praise my eyes and face?
And made your other love, Demetrius,
Who even but now did spurn me with his foot,                           225
To call me goddess, nymph, divine, and rare,
Precious, celestial? Wherefore speaks he this
To her he hates? And wherefore doth Lysander
Deny your love, so rich within his soul,[130]
And tender[131] me, forsooth! affection,[132]                          230
But by your setting on, by your consent?
What though I be not so in grace[133] as you,
So hung upon with love,[134] so fortunate?
But miserable most, to love unloved.[135]

99

136 *Make mouths upon* – "Make faces at" (twist the face into a mocking expression).

137 *hold . . . up* – "keep on with the joke you so much like".

138 *well carried* – "well carried out, performed".

139 *make me . . . argument* – "make me the subject for such a story (*argument*)".

140 *If . . . compel* – "If she (Helena) cannot persuade (Lysander, to leave her alone) I can force him to (*compel*)".

141 *by that . . . for thee* – i.e. "by my life".

142 *prove him false* – "prove that he lies".

This you should pity rather than despise.                     235

HERMIA

I understand not what you mean by this.

HELENA

Ay, do, perséver, counterfeit sad looks,
Make mouths upon[136] me when I turn my back,
Wink each at other, hold the sweet jest up:[137]
This sport, well carried,[138] shall be chronicled.          240
If you have any pity, grace, or manners,
You would not make me such an argument.[139]
But fare ye well; 't is partly my own fault,
Which death or absence soon shall remedy.

LYSANDER

Stay, gentle Helena, hear my excuse;                         245
My love, my life, my soul, fair Helena!

HELENA

O, excellent!

HERMIA

                    Sweet, do not scorn her so.

DEMETRIUS

If she cannot entreat, I can compel.[140]

LYSANDER

Thou canst compel no more than she entreat.
Thy threats have no more strength than her weak prayers.     250
Helen, I love thee, by my life I do;
I swear by that which I will lose for thee[141]
To prove him false[142] that says I love thee not.

101

143 *withdraw and prove it* Lysander is daring Demetrius to come away with him and fight for Helena. In the next line Demetrius accepts.

144 *whereto . . . this?* – "what is all this leading to?"

145 *Away, you Ethiope* (He struggles to break away from her). *Ethiope:* "Ethiopian" – only said because Hermia is darker than Helena.

146 *Seem to break loose* – "Make a show of trying to break away".

147 *take on as* – "pretend that".

148 *tame* – "weak"; "cowardly".

149 *Hang off* – "Do not hold on"; "Let go".

150 *thou cat, thou burr,* "cat", because of its claws; *burr:* a kind of plant whose seeds have hooks, which stick to clothes or hair and cannot be shaken off.

151 *tawny Tartar* – "dark-skinned Tartar" (see note 68). Hermia is called a "Tartar" for the same reason as she was called an "Ethiope".

DEMETRIUS

I say I love thee more than he can do.

LYSANDER

If thou say so, withdraw and prove it[143] too.                    255

DEMETRIUS

Quick, come.

HERMIA

                Lysander, whereto tends all this?[144]

LYSANDER

Away, you Ethiope.[145]

DEMETRIUS

                No, no, sir,
Seem to break loose;[146] take on as[147] you would follow,
But yet come not; you are a tame[148] man, go!

LYSANDER (*struggling with* HERMIA)

Hang off,[149] thou cat, thou burr;[150] vile thing, let loose,        260
Or I will shake thee from me like a serpent!

HERMIA

Why are you grown so rude? What change is this,
Sweet love?

LYSANDER

                Thy love? out, tawny Tartar,[151] out!
Out, loathéd medicine; hated potion, hence!

HERMIA

Do you not jest?

152 *Yes . . . do you.* Helena declares
that this quarrel is only a trick,
and that Hermia and Lysander are
still making fun of her. *Sooth :* "In
truth".

153 *I perceive . . . holds you.* The "weak
bond" is Hermia's arms holding
Lysander back. Demetrius con-
tinues to mock Lysander as a
coward. If Hermia's weak arms are
enough to bind him, then any
bond he enters into will also bind
him ; yet his *word* is not to be
trusted.

154 *what news –* "what new thing has
happened (to make you hate
me) ?"

155 *erewhile –* "a short time ago".

156 *since night –* "since this night
began".

157 *out . . . of question –* "with nothing
to hope for or argue about".

158 *canker-blossom,* flower of the wild
rose, like a garden rose except for
having no scent : hence, a person
whose appearance of beauty or
virtue is deceiving.

#### HELENA

Yes, sooth, and so do you.[152]                    265

#### LYSANDER

Demetrius, I will keep my word with thee.

#### DEMETRIUS

I would I had your bond; for I perceive
A weak bond holds you;[153] I 'll not trust your word.

#### LYSANDER

What, should I hurt her, strike her, kill her dead?
Although I hate her, I 'll not harm her so.                    270

#### HERMIA

What, can you do me greater harm than hate?
Hate me? Wherefore? O me, what news,[154] my love!
Am not I Hermia? Are not you Lysander?
I am as fair now as I was erewhile.[155]
Since night[156] you loved me; yet since night you left me.    275
Why then, you left me – O, the gods forbid! –
In earnest, shall I say?

#### LYSANDER

                         Ay, by my life:
And never did desire to see thee more.
Therefore be out of hope, of question,[157] of doubt;
Be certain, nothing truer, 't is no jest                    280
That I do hate thee, and love Helena.

#### HERMIA

O me! you juggler, you canker-blossom,[158]
You thief of love! What, have you come by night
And stolen my love's heart from him?

E                                    105

159 *i' faith* – "in faith"; "indeed".
160 *touch* – "quality in your character".
161 *tear impatient answers . . . tongue* – "force me, gentle as I am in speech (*tongue*), to answer you impatiently".
162 *counterfeit* – "imitation of a woman"; i.e. deceiver.
163 *puppet*, model of a person, used in a kind of play where such little models act the parts of human beings.
164 *that way . . . game* – "that is the direction your thoughts are following". *game*: birds or beasts to be hunted; as if Helena's thoughts are following the idea of smallness like a hunter pursuing game.

165 *personage* – "bodily appearance"; "figure".
166 *prevailed* – "triumphed" (over Hermia).
167 *so high in his esteem* – "so high in his opinion of you" (Hermia plays on the idea of Helena's height right through this speech).
168 *thou painted maypole* (see "maypole"). Mocking at the tall Helena.
169 *I am not yet . . . eyes*, i.e. a threat to scratch Helena's eyes.
170 *curst* – "bad-natured"; "wishing harm".
171 *no gift . . . shrewishness* – "no natural ability at all in scolding".
172 *a right maid* – "very much a girl".
173 *hark* – "listen".

*thou painted maypole* [168]

#### HELENA

Fine, i' faith!¹⁵⁹
Have you no modesty, no maiden shame,                        285
No touch¹⁶⁰ of bashfulness? What, will you tear
Impatient answers from my gentle tongue?¹⁶¹
Fie, fie, you counterfeit,¹⁶² you puppet,¹⁶³ you!

#### HERMIA

Puppet? why so! Ay, that way goes the game.¹⁶⁴
Now I perceive that she hath made compare                    290
Between our statures; she hath urged her height,
And with her personage, her tall personage,¹⁶⁵
Her height, forsooth, she hath prevailed¹⁶⁶ with him.
And are you grown so high in his esteem¹⁶⁷
Because I am so dwarfish and so low?                         295
How low am I, thou painted maypole?¹⁶⁸ Speak,
How low am I? I am not yet so low
But that my nails can reach unto thine eyes.¹⁶⁹

#### HELENA

I pray you, though you mock me, gentlemen,
Let her not hurt me. I was never curst;¹⁷⁰                   300
I have no gift at all in shrewishness;¹⁷¹
I am a right maid¹⁷² for my cowardice;
Let her not strike me: you perhaps may think,
Because she is something lower than myself,
That I can match her.

#### HERMIA

"Lower"! hark,¹⁷³ again!                                     305

#### HELENA

Good Hermia, do not be so bitter with me.
I evermore did love you, Hermia,
Did ever keep your counsels, never wronged you;
Save that, in love unto Demetrius,

174 *stealth* – "secret flight".
175 *so* – "on condition that".
176 *bear my folly back* – "take my foolish love back".
177 *simple* – "harmless"; "innocent".

178 *fond* – "foolish".
179 *take her part* – "side with her".
180 *shrewd* – "shrewish".
181 *suffer* – "allow".

I told him of your stealth[174] unto this wood.                    310
He followed you; for love I followed him;
But he hath chid me hence and threatened me
To strike me, spurn me, nay, to kill me too.
And now, so[175] you will let me quiet go,
To Athens will I bear my folly back,[176]                         315
And follow you no further. Let me go.
You see how simple[177] and how fond[178] I am.

### HERMIA

Why, get you gone! who is 't that hinders you?

### HELENA

A foolish heart, that I leave here behind.

### HERMIA

What, with Lysander?

### HELENA

                     With Demetrius.                    320

### LYSANDER

Be not afraid, she shall not harm thee, Helena.

### DEMETRIUS

No, sir, she shall not, though you take her part.[179]

### HELENA

O, when she 's angry, she is keen and shrewd.[180]
She was a vixen when she went to school;
And though she be but little, she is fierce.                       325

### HERMIA

Little again? nothing but low and little?
Why will you suffer[181] her to flout me thus?
Let me come to her.

182 *minimus* – "smallest thing" (from Latin).
183 *knot-grass* – a kind of weed with twisted stems that hold back the feet – i.e. she is a little person who gets in the way.
184 *officious* – "dutiful".
185 *in her behalf* – "in support of her (Helena)".
186 *Never so little* – "However little".
187 *aby* – see note 104.
188 *whose right . . . in Helena* – "who has more right to Helena, you or I?".

189 *cheek by jowl* – "cheek to cheek" (a common expression, meaning "side by side").
190 *coil* – "disturbance".
191 *'long of* – (= *along of*) "because of".
192 *Your hands than mine . . . run away* – "Your hands are quicker than mine in a fight, but my legs, being longer, can run away faster".

#### LYSANDER

              Get you gone, you dwarf,
You minimus,[182] of hindering knot-grass[183] made,
You bead, you acorn.

#### DEMETRIUS

              You are too officious[184]    330
In her behalf[185] that scorns your services.
Let her alone; speak not of Helena;
Take not her part. For if thou dost intend
Never so little[186] show of love to her,
Thou shalt aby[187] it.

#### LYSANDER

              Now she holds me not.    335
Now follow, if thou dar'st, to try whose right,
Of thine or mine, is most in Helena.[188]

#### DEMETRIUS

Follow? Nay, I 'll go with thee cheek by jowl.[189]
           [*Exeunt* LYSANDER *and* DEMETRIUS

#### HERMIA

You, mistress, all this coil[190] is 'long of[191] you.
Nay, go not back.

#### HELENA

             I will not trust you, I    340
Nor longer stay in your curst company.
Your hands than mine are quicker for a fray,
My legs are longer, though, to run away.[192]    [*Exit*

#### HERMIA

I am amazed, and know not what to say.

           [*Exit*

193 *commit'st thy knaveries wilfully* – "you do your bad deeds on purpose (*wilfully*)".

194 *shadows* – "spirits".

195 *'nointed* – (= *anointed* q.v.).

196 *sort* – "turn out"; "happen".

197 *As this . . . sport* – "Since this quarrelling of theirs (*jangling*) I consider as an amusement (*sport*)".

198 *Hie* – "Go".

199 *overcast the night* – "make the night dark with clouds".

200 *welkin* – "sky".

201 *drooping* – "low-lying".

202 *Acheron*, an imaginary river of deep, black water in Hades, the underworld country to which – as the ancient Greeks believed – men's souls went after death.

203 *Like to . . . thy tongue* – "change your voice (*frame thy tongue*) at times so that it sounds like Lysander's".

204 *rail thou* – "speak insultingly".

205 *from* – "away from".

206 *death-counterfeiting sleep* – "sleep which imitates death in appearance".

207 *with leaden legs* – "moving as heavily as if its legs were of lead". The image is of sleep like some slow, heavy creature that creeps over the eyes.

208 *batty wings* – "wings like a bat's".

209 *liquor* – "juice".

210 *virtuous property* – "special power" ("virtue" in a plant was its natural power of healing).

211 *from thence*, i.e. from his eye.

212 *his* (the herb's).

213 *And make . . . sight* – "And make his eyes look around him (*eyeballs roll*) with their usual (*wonted*) sight" (and not charmed, as before).

214 *wend* – "go".

215 *league* – "friendship".

OBERON *and* PUCK *come forward*

OBERON

This is thy negligence; still thou mistak'st;                    345
Or else committ'st thy knaveries wilfully.[193]

PUCK

Believe me, king of shadows,[194] I mistook.
Did not you tell me I should know the man
By the Athenian garments he had on?
And so far blameless proves my enterprise                        350
That I have 'nointed[195] an Athenian's eyes;
And so far am I glad it so did sort,[196]
As this their jangling I esteem a sport.[197]

OBERON

Thou seest these lovers seek a place to fight.
Hie,[198] therefore, Robin, overcast the night;[199]             355
The starry welkin[200] cover thou anon
With drooping[201] fog as black as Acheron;[202]
And lead these testy rivals so astray
As one come not within another's way.
Like to Lysander sometime frame thy tongue,[203]                360
Then stir Demetrius up with bitter wrong;
And sometime rail thou[204] like Demetrius;
And from[205] each other look thou lead them thus,
Till o'er their brows death-counterfeiting sleep[206]
With leaden legs[207] and batty wings[208] doth creep;           365
Then crush this herb into Lysander's eye;
Whose liquor[209] hath this virtuous property,[210]
To take from thence[211] all error with his[212] might
And make his eyeballs roll with wonted sight.[213]
When they next wake, all this derision                           370
Shall seem a dream, and fruitless vision;
And back to Athens shall the lovers wend,[214]
With league[215] whose date till death shall never end.

216 *I'll to* – "I'll go to".

217 *her charméd . . . view* – "set free her sight, which had been charmed, so that she will not have to view a monster (i.e. Bottom with the ass's head)".

218 *night's swift dragons . . . fast* – "night is quickly passing from the cloudy sky". Shakespeare here imagines night as a goddess driven across the sky by dragons (q.v.) with dark wings.

219 *Aurora's harbinger* – "the morning star which appears before sunrise". *Aurora:* Roman goddess of the sunrise; *harbinger:* one who comes before a great person to prepare the way.

220 *crossways* – "places where two or more roads cross". Persons who killed themselves were buried there.

221 *wormy beds* – "graves" (where worms are to be found).

222 *They wilfully . . . light* – "Of their own will (*wilfully*) they (the "damned spirits") choose to live away from the light of day".

223 *for aye consort* – "for ever keep company (*consort*)".

224 *spirits of another sort* (not like those which fear the day-light). While the ghosts of the damned vanish at the first sign of day, the fairies may walk until the sun is fully risen.

225 *the morning's love*, i.e. Aurora. See note 219.

226 *the groves may tread* – "may walk in the woods".

227 *the eastern gate* – "the place in the eastern sky where the rising sun enters".

228 *Opening on Neptune* – "Opening on to the sea". Neptune was god of the sea; hence, the sea itself.

229 *beams* – "beams of sunlight".

230 *his* (the sea's).

231 *haste* – "hasten"; "make haste".

232 *effect* – "complete".

233 *in field and town* – "both in the country and in the town".

234 *Goblin* (see glossary), i.e. Puck himself.

114

Whiles I in this affair do thee employ,
I 'll to[216] my Queen, and beg her Indian boy;               375
And then I will her charméd eye release
From monster's view,[217] and all things shall be peace.

PUCK

My fairy lord, this must be done with haste,
For night's swift dragons cut the clouds full fast,[218]
And yonder shines Aurora's harbinger;[219]                    380
At whose approach, ghosts wandering here and there,
Troop home to churchyards. Damnéd spirits all,
That in crossways[220] and floods have burial,
Already to their wormy beds[221] are gone;
For fear lest day should look their shames upon,             385
They wilfully themselves exile from light,[222]
And must for aye consort[223] with black-browed night.

OBERON

But we are spirits of another sort:[224]
I with the morning's love[225] have oft made sport,
And, like a forester, the groves may tread[226]               390
Even till the eastern gate,[227] all fiery-red,
Opening on Neptune,[228] with fair blesséd beams[229]
Turns into yellow gold his[230] salt green streams.
But notwithstanding, haste,[231] make no delay:
We may effect[232] this business yet ere day.                 395
                                        [*Exit* OBERON

PUCK

Up and down, up and down,
I will lead them up and down;
I am feared in field and town;[233]
Goblin,[234] lead them up and down.
Here comes one.                                               400

*Enter* LYSANDER

235 *Here, villain* – Puck imitates the voice of Demetrius to mislead Lysander.

236 *drawn and ready* – "with sword drawn, ready to fight".

237 *plainer* – "more level".

238 *Thou coward*, etc. Here, and in the rest of his speeches up to Helena's entrance, Puck imitates Lysander's voice to Demetrius.

239 *to the stars* – "to the empty night".

240 *recreant* – "coward".

241 *we 'll . . . here* – "we shall not try out here which of us is the more manly", i.e. "we shall not have the fight here".

LYSANDER

Where art thou, proud Demetrius? Speak thou now.

PUCK (*as* DEMETRIUS)

Here villain,[235] drawn and ready.[236] Where art thou?

LYSANDER

I will be with thee straight.

PUCK (*as* DEMETRIUS)

               Follow me, then,
To plainer[237] ground.

                        [*Exit* LYSANDER

*Enter* DEMETRIUS

DEMETRIUS

               Lysander, speak again;
Thou runaway, thou coward, art thou fled?         405
Speak! In some bush? Where dost thou hide thy head?

PUCK (*as* LYSANDER)

Thou coward,[238] art thou bragging to the stars,[239]
Telling the bushes that thou look'st for wars,
And wilt not come? Come, recreant,[240] come, thou child;
I 'll whip thee with a rod. He is defiled         410
That draws a sword on thee.

DEMETRIUS

                 Yea, art thou there?

PUCK (*as* LYSANDER)

Follow my voice; we 'll try no manhood here.[241]

                        [*Exeunt*

*Re-enter* LYSANDER
117

242 *lighter-heeled* – "quicker at running".

243 *That* – "So that".

244 *fallen am I . . . way* – Lysander can feel with his feet the slope of the fairy bank, but he cannot see it in the dark. *fallen am I*: "I find myself" (not "I have fallen").

245 *spite* – "insult".

246 *Abide me* – "Wait for me".

247 *wot* – "know".

248 *shifting every place* – "moving constantly from place to place".

249 *buy this dear* – "pay dearly (be heavily punished) for this mockery" (*buy* has the same meaning as "aby").

250 *To measure . . . bed* – "To lie full length on this cold ground (*bed*)".

251 *visited*, by Demetrius, so as to proceed with the fight; or, punished by him.

#### LYSANDER

He goes before me, and still dares me on;
When I come where he calls, then he is gone.
The villain is much lighter-heeled[242] than I:                    415
I followed fast, but faster he did fly,
That[243] fallen am I in dark uneven way,[244]
And here will rest me. Come, thou gentle day;

                                    *[Lies down*

For if but once thou show me thy grey light,
I 'll find Demetrius, and revenge this spite.[245] *(Sleeps)*          420


#### *Re-enter* PUCK *and* DEMETRIUS


#### PUCK (*as* LYSANDER)

Ho, ho, ho! coward, why com'st thou not?


#### DEMETRIUS

Abide me,[246] if thou dar'st; for well I wot,[247]
Thou runn'st before me, shifting every place,[248]
And dar'st not stand, nor look me in the face.
Where art thou now?


#### PUCK (*as* LYSANDER)

                    Come hither, I am here.          425


#### DEMETRIUS

Nay, then, thou mock'st me; thou shalt buy this dear,[249]
If ever I thy face by daylight see.
Now, go thy way: faintness constraineth me
To measure out my length on this cold bed:[250]
By day's approach look to be visited.[251]          430

                            *[Lies down and sleeps*


#### *Enter* HELENA

252 *Abate thy hours* – "Reduce (*abate*) the number of hours (of night)".
253 *sorrow's eye* – "the eyes of those who know sorrow".
254 *but three*. Demetrius, Lysander and Helena have lain down to sleep, none knowing in the dark that the others are so near.

255 *curst* – "angry".
256 *Bedabbled* – "Made wet and dirty".
257 *My legs . . . desires* – "I cannot walk as fast as my desires would like me to move". *keep pace with*: keep up with in walking.
258 *tak'st* – "will take".

#### HELENA

O weary night, O long and tedious night,
Abate thy hours,[252] shine comforts from the east,
That I may back to Athens by daylight,
From these that my poor company detest;
And sleep, that sometimes shuts up sorrow's eye,[253]          435
Steal me awhile from mine own company.

[*Lies down and sleeps*

#### PUCK

Yet but three?[254] Come one more.
Two of both kinds makes up four.
Here she comes, curst[255] and sad;
Cupid is a knavish lad,                                       440
Thus to make poor females mad.

*Enter* HERMIA

#### HERMIA

Never so weary, never so in woe,
Bedabbled[256] with the dew, and torn with briers,
I can no further crawl, no further go;
My legs can keep no pace with my desires.[257]                445
Here will I rest me till the break of day.
Heavens shield Lysander, if they mean a fray!

[*Lies down and sleeps*

#### PUCK

On the ground
Sleep sound;
I 'll apply                                                    450
To your eye,
Gentle lover, remedy.   [*Squeezes the juice on* LYSANDER'S *eyes*
When thou wak'st,
Thou tak'st[258]
True delight                                                   455

121

259 *That every . . . own* – "That every man should take a wife for himself".

260 *In your waking* – "When you wake up".

261 *Jack shall have Jill* – "Each young man shall win his girl". (Jack being a common name for a man, Jill for a girl; hence "Jack" = any male, "Jill" = any female).

262 *The man shall have his mare again.* Another proverb, meaning much the same as "Jack shall have Jill".

In the sight
Of thy former lady's eye;
And the country proverb known,
That every man should take his own,[259]
In your waking[260] shall be shown. 460
Jack shall have Jill;[261]
Nought shall go ill;
The man shall have his mare again,[262] and all shall be well.

                           *[Exit*
                     *[The lovers lie asleep*

(iv.i) Titania and Bottom enter, attended by the fairies. They fall asleep. Oberon and Puck see them: Titania has given up the boy about whom they had quarrelled, and Oberon now removes the charm. Titania wakes up, in love again with her husband, and they go away happily together.

It is now morning. Theseus and Hippolyta enter with Egeus: they are up early, to celebrate May Day. The lovers awaken, Lysander in love with Hermia, Demetrius with Helena. Theseus decides that they shall all be married on his own wedding day.

Bottom wakes up, amazed at the dream he has had.

1 *coy* – "smooth with the hand"; "stroke".

2 *stick* – "fix as an ornament".

3 *Monsieur* – "Master"; "Mister". (French)

4 *fret* – "worry"; but *fret* also means "wear away" – which would destroy a cobweb.

5 *overflown with* – "flooded by".

6 *neaf* – "fist" (i.e. "shake hands").

7 *leave your curtsy* – "stop bowing" (Mustardseed keeps bowing ceremoniously to Bottom).

# ACT FOUR

*Scene I. The same place.*

*Enter* TITANIA *and* BOTTOM, *with the fairies attending,*
*and* OBERON *behind, unseen.*

### TITANIA

Come, sit thee down upon this flowery bed,
While I thy amiable cheeks do coy,[1]
And stick[2] musk-roses in thy sleek smooth head,
And kiss thy fair large ears, my gentle joy.

### BOTTOM

Where 's Peaseblossom?                                                            5

### PEASEBLOSSOM

Ready.

### BOTTOM

Scratch my head, Peaseblossom. Where 's Monsieur[3] Cobweb?

### COBWEB

Ready.

### BOTTOM

Monsieur Cobweb, good monsieur, get you your weapons
in your hand, and kill me a red-hipped humble-bee on the top   10
of a thistle; and good monsieur, bring me the honey-bag. Do
not fret[4] yourself too much in the action, monsieur; and good
monsieur, have a care the honey-bag break not; I would be
loth to have you overflown[5] with a honey-bag, signior.
Where 's Monsieur Mustardseed?                                                    15

### MUSTARDSEED

Ready.

### BOTTOM

Give me your neaf,[6] Monsieur Mustardseed. Pray you, leave
your curtsy,[7] good monsieur.

8 *Cavalery* – "knight"; "noble-man" (from Italian *cavaliere*; the usual English form is "cavalier").

9 *a reasonable . . . music* – "a fair ability to enjoy music" (*ear* draws attention to the ass's ears on Bottom's head).

10 *the tongs and the bones* – rough musical instruments used in the country.

11 *bottle* – "bundle".

12 *hath no fellow* – "has nothing to equal it". Bottom's likings in food have changed to suit his ass's head).

13 *hoard* – "store" (see "squirrel").

14 *exposition*. He means a "disposition" or desire.

15 *wind . . . arms* – "wrap my arms around you".

16 *be all ways away* – "go away in all directions".

*The squirrel's hoard* [13]

#### MUSTARDSEED

What 's your will?

#### BOTTOM

Nothing, good monsieur, but to help Cavalery[8] Cobweb to    20
scratch. I must to the barber's, monsieur, for methinks I am
marvellous hairy about the face. And I am such a tender ass, if
my hair do but tickle me, I must scratch.

#### TITANIA

What, wilt thou hear some music, my sweet love?

#### BOTTOM

I have a reasonable good ear in music.[9] Let 's have the tongs and    25
the bones.[10]

#### TITANIA

Or say, sweet love, what thou desirest to eat.

#### BOTTOM

Truly, a peck of provender; I could munch your good dry oats.
Methinks I have a great desire to a bottle[11] of hay: good hay,
sweet hay, hath no fellow.[12]    30

#### TITANIA

I have a venturous fairy, that shall seek
The squirrel's hoard,[13] and fetch thee thence new nuts.

#### BOTTOM

I had rather have a handful or two of dried peas. But I pray you,
let none of your people stir me; I have an exposition[14] of sleep
come upon me.    35

#### TITANIA

Sleep thou, and I will wind thee in my arms.[15]
Fairies, be gone, and be all ways away.[16]

[*Exeunt Fairies*

17 *entwist* – "twist itself round".
Woodbine and honeysuckle are two names for the same plant: it is impossible to say which "entwists" which. But "woodbine" may be a mistake for "bindweed", another climbing plant.
18 *female* – "behaving like a female".
19 *Enrings* – "Grows round in a ring"; "Surrounds".
20 *barky fingers* – "small, finger-shaped branches covered with bark (q.v.)".
21 *this sweet sight*, i.e. Titania and Bottom lying asleep together.
22 *dotage* – "doting state of mind"; "foolish love".
23 *favours* – see note 7 to II.i.
24 *fall out with* – "quarrel with".
25 *she . . . rounded* – "she had then made a circle round his hairy temples" (q.v.).
26 (lines 49–51) *And that same . . . eyes.* Oberon describes the tears in Titania's eyes. They were shaped like the dew-drops that usually form (*wont to swell*) on buds – looking like round, precious pearls (see "orient") – but as if such "dew-drop" tears stood now within pretty little flowers (*flowerets*), i.e. her eyes.

27 *at my pleasure* – "as much as I liked".
28 *terms* – "words".
29 *her changeling child,* i.e. the same as described, II.i.120 and on.
30 *her fairy sent* – "sent her fairy".
31 *undo* – "remove".
32 *imperfection* – "fault".
33 *transforméd scalp* – "skin of the head (*scalp*) changed (*transformed*) into that of an ass".
34 *swain* – "country lover".
35 *repair* – "return".
36 *accidents* – "unexpected happenings".
37 *wont to be* – "used to being".

So doth the woodbine the sweet honeysuckle
Gently entwist;[17] the female[18] ivy so
Enrings[19] the barky fingers[20] of the elm.                          40
O, how I love thee! how I dote on thee!

[*They sleep*

*Enter* PUCK

OBERON (*coming forward*)

Welcome, good Robin: seest thou this sweet sight?[21]
Her dotage[22] now I do begin to pity;
For meeting her of late behind the wood,
Seeking sweet favours[23] for this hateful fool,                        45
I did upbraid her, and fall out with[24] her.
For she his hairy temples then had rounded[25]
With coronet of fresh and fragrant flowers;
And that same dew, which sometime on the buds
Was wont to swell like round and orient pearls,                         50
Stood now within the pretty flowerets' eyes,[26]
Like tears that did their own disgrace bewail.
When I had at my pleasure[27] taunted her,
And she in mild terms[28] begged my patience,
I then did ask of her her changeling child;[29]                         55
Which straight she gave me, and her fairy sent[30]
To bear him to my bower in fairy land.
And now I have the boy, I will undo[31]
This hateful imperfection[32] of her eyes.
And, gentle Puck, take this transforméd scalp,[33]                      60
From off the head of this Athenian swain,[34]
That he awaking when the other do,
May all to Athens back again repair,[35]
And think no more of this night's accidents[36]
But as the fierce vexation of a dream.                                  65
But first I will release the Fairy Queen.

[*Touches* TITANIA's *eyelids*

Be as thou wast wont to be;[37]
See as thou wast wont to see.

129

38 *Dian's bud . . . power* – "Chastity, whose sign is the closed bud of Diana, the maiden goddess, has more power than love, whose sign is the open flower of Cupid".

39 *this head,* the ass-head on Bottom, which can easily be taken off

40 *strike more dead . . . sense* – "strike the senses of all five (the four lovers and Bottom) more dead (i.e. unconscious) than ordinary sleep could".

41 *peep* – "look out".

42 *sound music* – "let music sound".

43 *rock the ground* – "make the ground shake".

44 *new in amity* – "made friends again". *amity* : friendship.

45 *solemnly* – "with full ceremony".

46 *triumphantly* – "in state".

47 *to* – "with".

130

> Dian's bud o'er Cupid's flower
> Hath such force and blessed power.[38]  70
Now, my Titania, wake you, my sweet Queen.

#### TITANIA (*wakes and rises*)

My Oberon! What visions have I seen!
Methought I was enamoured of an ass.

#### OBERON

There lies your love.

#### TITANIA

                    How came these things to pass?
O, how mine eyes do loathe his visage now!  75

#### OBERON

Silence awhile. Robin, take off this head;[39]
Titania, music call, and strike more dead
Than common sleep, of all these five the sense.[40]

#### TITANIA

Music, ho music, such as charmeth sleep!

[*Music plays*

#### PUCK

Now, when thou wak'st, with thine own fool's eyes peep.[41]  80

#### OBERON

Sound, music;[42] come, my Queen, take hands with me,
And rock the ground[43] whereon these sleepers be.
Now thou and I are new in amity,[44]
And will tomorrow midnight solemnly[45]
Dance in Duke Theseus' house triumphantly,[46]  85
And bless it to[47] all fair prosperity.
There shall the pairs of faithful lovers be
Wedded, with Theseus, all in jollity.

48 *attend and mark* – "listen and take notice".
49 *the morning lark* – "the lark singing in the early morning".
50 *Trip . . . shade* – "Let us dance away with the shadow of night". *nightes*: compare with "moones", II.i.7 and note.
51 *came* – "happened".
52 *observation*, keeping the ancient ceremonies of May Day (see note 107 to I.i).
53 *vaward of the day* – "the early hours of the day". *vaward* = vanguard, the soldiers in the front ranks of an army; hence this image of the first hours of the advancing day.
54 *music of my hounds* – "the pleasant sound of my hunting dogs (giving cry in the distance)".
55 *Uncouple* – "Set (the dogs) loose".
56 *Dispatch* – "Hurry".
57 *the musical confusion . . . conjunction* – "the pleasant mixture of sounds made by the dogs' cries together with the echoes of these cries". This describes a familiar experience for country people in Shakespeare's time.
58 *Hercules*, a Greek hero in ancient stories, famous for his strength.
59 *Cadmus*, believed to have founded the Greek city of Thebes and taught his people how to write.
60 *Crete*, a large island off the coast of Greece.
61 *bayed the bear* – "hunted the bear".
62 *Sparta*, a famous Greek city in ancient times.
63 *gallant chiding* – "brave (*gallant*), angry cries".

*Hunting horns sound*

132

PUCK

Fairy King, attend and mark;[48]
I do hear the morning lark.[49]                                    90

OBERON

Then, my Queen, in silence sad
Trip we after nightes shade;[50]
We the globe can compass soon,
Swifter than the wandering moon.

TITANIA

Come, my lord, and in our flight                                   95
Tell me how it came[51] this night
That I sleeping here was found,
With these mortals on the ground.

[*Exeunt. The lovers and* BOTTOM *sleep on*

*Hunting horns sound. Enter* THESEUS, HIPPOLYTA, EGEUS,
*and their train*

THESEUS

Go one of you, find out the forester,
For now our observation[52] is performed;                          100
And since we have the vaward of the day,[53]
My love shall hear the music of my hounds.[54]
Uncouple[55] in the western valley; let them go;
Dispatch,[56] I say, and find the forester. [*Exit an Attendant*
We will, fair queen, up to the mountain's top,                     105
And mark the musical confusion
Of hounds and echo in conjunction.[57]

HIPPOLYTA

I was with Hercules[58] and Cadmus[59] once,
When in a wood of Crete[60] they bayed the bear[61]
With hounds of Sparta;[62] never did I hear                        110
Such gallant chiding;[63] for, besides the groves,

133

64 *one mutual cry*, cries made by each
answering the other (*mutual*), so
that all the cries from different
places combined into one.

65 *sweet thunder* – "a loud noise like
thunder, yet beautiful".

66 *flewed* – "with large cheeks hanging down".

67 *sanded* – "sand-coloured".

68 *sweep . . . dew*, i.e. ears that fall so
close to the ground as to brush the
morning dew away.

69 *Crook-kneed* – "With bent knees".

70 *dew-lapped* – "with loose skin
hanging from the throat".

71 *Thessalian*, from Thessaly, a
district to the north of Greece.

72 *matched in mouth . . . each* – "their
cries sounding in tune, like church
bells with different tones sounding
together (*each under each*)". Elizabethan gentlemen often chose their
hunting dogs for this quality.

73 *tuneable* – "tuneful"; "musical".

74 *holla'd to* – "shouted to" (in reply,
by the hunters following the
hounds).

75 *horn* – "hunting-horn" (blown to
call the hunters together).

76 *soft* – "speak quietly".

77 *of* – "at".

78 *to observe The rite of May* – (see
note 107 to I.i).

79 *intent* – "intention" (of keeping
May Day).

80 *in grace of our solemnity* – "to do
honour to our ceremony".

81 *morrow* – "morning".

82 *Saint Valentine is past.* Saint
Valentine's Day, February 14th,
was believed to be the time when
the birds chose their lovers.

83 *these wood-birds*, i.e. the four lovers
in the wood.

84 *to couple* – "to form pairs".

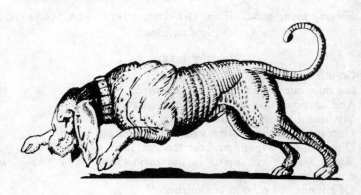

*their heads are hung*
*With ears that sweep away the morning dew* [68]

The skies, the fountains, every region near
Seemed all one mutual cry.[64] I never heard
So musical a discord, such sweet thunder.[65]

THESEUS

My hounds are bred out of the Spartan kind,                    115
So flewed,[66] so sanded,[67] and their heads are hung
With ears that sweep away the morning dew,[68]
Crook-kneed[69] and dew-lapped,[70] like Thessalian bulls;[71]
Slow in pursuit, but matched in mouth like bells,
Each under each.[72] A cry more tuneable[73]                   120
Was never holla'd to,[74] nor cheered with horn,[75]
In Crete, in Sparta, nor in Thessaly.
Judge when you hear. But soft,[76] what nymphs are these?

EGEUS

My lord, this is my daughter here asleep,
And this Lysander, this Demetrius is,                          125
This Helena, old Nedar's Helena;
I wonder of[77] their being here together.

THESEUS

No doubt they rose up early to observe
The rite of May;[78] and, hearing our intent,[79]
Came here in grace of our solemnity.[80]                       130
But speak, Egeus; is not this the day
That Hermia should give answer of her choice?

EGEUS

It is, my lord.

THESEUS

Go bid the huntsmen wake them with their horns.

*Horns sound. A shout within. The lovers wake up.*

Good morrow,[81] friends! Saint Valentine is past:[82]        135
Begin these wood-birds[83] but to couple[84] now?

135

85 *is so far from* – "has so little to do with".
86 *To sleep by hate* – "(As) to sleep near a person who hates you".
87 *amazedly* – "in a confused way".
88 *Half sleep, half waking* – "Half asleep, half awake".
89 *bethink me* – "remember".
90 *Without the peril of* – "Away from the danger of".

91 *you have enough* – "you have heard enough".
92 *defeated* – "cheated".
93 *stealth* – "stealing away"; "secret flight".
94 *purpose hither* – "purpose to come here".
95 *in fancy* – "because of her love".

LYSANDER

Pardon, my lord.                              [*The lovers kneel*

THESEUS

                        I pray you all, stand up.
I know you two are rival enemies.
How comes this gentle concord in the world,
That hatred is so far from[85] jealousy                         140
To sleep by hate,[86] and fear no enmity?

LYSANDER

My lord, I shall reply amazédly,[87]
Half sleep, half waking.[88] But as yet, I swear,
I cannot truly say how I came here.
But as I think, for truly would I speak,                        145
And now I do bethink me,[89] so it is:
I came with Hermia hither: our intent
Was to be gone from Athens, where we might,
Without the peril[90] of the Athenian law—

EGEUS

Enough, enough, my lord; you have enough;[91]                   150
I beg the law, the law, upon his head.
They would have stolen away; they would, Demetrius,
Thereby to have defeated[92] you and me:
You of your wife, and me of my consent;
Of my consent, that she should be your wife.                    155

DEMETRIUS

My lord, fair Helen told me of their stealth,[93]
Of this their purpose hither[94] to this wood,
And I in fury hither followed them;
Fair Helena in fancy[95] following me.
But, my good lord, I wot not by what power,                     160
But by some power it is, my love to Hermia,
Melted as doth the snow, seems to me now

F                          137

96 *an idle gaud* – "a foolish toy".

97 *But like in sickness . . . taste.* Demetrius compares his feelings towards Helena with those of a man who hates some kind of food when he is ill; once he is well again, he gets his natural taste back and likes what he enjoyed before.

98 *overbear your will* – "over-rule (refuse to grant) your wishes".

99 *by and by* – "soon".

100 *knit* – "bound together (in marriage)".

101 *for* – "because".

102 *the morning . . . worn* – "the freshness of the morning has now rather worn away"; i.e. "it is now getting rather late in the morning".

103 *three and three* – "three sets of couples" (including Theseus and Hippolyta).

104 *undistinguishable* – "the details not to be distinguished (in memory)".

105 *Like far-off mountains . . . clouds* – "Like mountains so far off that they look like clouds".

106 *with parted eye* – "with eyes that are not focussed", i.e. where each eye sees the object separately, giving a double view.

107 *I have found . . . own.* Demetrius seems like a jewel Helena has found. It may have some owner to come and claim it; she cannot be sure that the "jewel" (Demetrius) is hers to keep.

As the remembrance of an idle gaud,[96]
Which in my childhood I did dote upon;
And all the faith, the virtue of my heart,                    165
The object and the pleasure of mine eye,
Is only Helena. To her, my lord,
Was I betrothed ere I saw Hermia;
But like in sickness did I loathe this food;
But, as in health, come to my natural taste,[97]              170
Now I do wish it, love it, long for it,
And will for evermore be true to it.

#### THESEUS

Fair lovers, you are fortunately met;
Of this discourse we more will hear anon.
Egeus, I will overbear your will,[98]                         175
For in the temple, by and by,[99] with us
These couples shall eternally be knit.[100]
And, for[101] the morning now is something worn,[102]
Our purposed hunting shall be set aside.
Away with us to Athens; three and three,[103]                 180
We 'll hold a feast in great solemnity.
Come, Hippolyta.

> [*Exeunt all but the lovers and* BOTTOM, *still asleep*

#### DEMETRIUS

These things seem small and undistinguishable,[104]
Like far-off mountains turnéd into clouds.[105]

#### HERMIA

Methinks I see these things with parted eye,[106]             185
When every thing seems double.

#### HELENA
                              So methinks;
And I have found Demetrius, like a jewel,
Mine own, and not mine own.[107]

108 *My next* – "The next 'cue' for me".
109 *Heigh-ho*, a yawn.
110 *God's my life!* – "God bless me!"
111 *rare* – "wonderful".
112 *an ass* – "a fool" (the word "ass" reminds the audience of what happened to Bottom).
113 *methought I had.* Bottom does not complete the sentence. It is, of course, the ass's head that he "had".
114 *a patched fool* – "like the Fool in a play" (*patched*: see note 6 to III.ii).

115 *The eye of man hath not heard.* Throughout this sentence, Bottom gets his expressions mixed.
116 *in the latter end* – "at the very end". It was quite usual for a comic play to end with a song; as does *A Midsummer Night's Dream*.
117 *Peradventure* – "Perhaps".
118 *gracious* – "pleasing".
119 *at her death,* i.e. at the death of Thisbe, in the play Bottom had been rehearsing.

#### DEMETRIUS

Are you sure
That we are awake? It seems to me
That yet we sleep, we dream. Do not you think      190
The Duke was here, and bid us follow him?

#### HERMIA

Yea, and my father.

#### HELENA

And Hippolyta.

#### LYSANDER

And he did bid us follow to the temple.

#### DEMETRIUS

Why then, we are awake; let 's follow him,
And by the way let us recount our dreams.      195

[*Exeunt the lovers*

#### BOTTOM (*waking up*)

When my cue comes, call me, and I will answer. My next[108] is
"Most fair Pyramus". Heigh-ho![109] Peter Quince! Flute the
bellows-mender! Snout the tinker! Starveling! God 's my
life![110] Stolen hence, and left me asleep! I have had a most
rare[111] vision. I have had a dream, past the wit of man to say      200
what dream it was. Man is but an ass[112] if he go about to
expound this dream. Methought I was – there is no man can tell
what. Methought I was, and methought I had[113] – but man is
but a patched fool,[114] if he will offer to say what methought I
had. The eye of man hath not heard,[115] the ear of man hath not      205
seen, man's hand is not able to taste, his tongue to conceive, nor
his heart to report, what my dream was. I will get Peter Quince
to write a ballad of this dream; it shall be called "Bottom's
Dream", because it hath no bottom; and I will sing it in the
latter end[116] of a play, before the Duke. Peradventure,[117] to      210
make it the more gracious,[118] I shall sing it at her death.[119]

[*Exit*

(IV.ii) The companions of Bottom are gathered together, waiting for him. He joins them and tells them to be ready with their play.

1 *Out of doubt* – "Without doubt"; "Surely".
2 *transported* – "out of his senses" (or perhaps, "carried away").
3 *goes not forward* – "does not make progress".
4 *discharge* – "perform".
5 *person* – "bodily appearance"; "figure".

6 *paramour* – "lover"; but, as Flute points out, he means "paragon" (q.v.).
7 *a thing of naught* – "a wicked person".
8 *If our sport . . . forward* – "If our entertainment had been ready".
9 *made men* – "men whose future success is 'made', or sure".

## Scene II. Athens.

*Enter* QUINCE, FLUTE, SNOUT, *and* STARVELING.

### QUINCE
Have you sent to Bottom's house? Is he come home yet?

### STARVELING
He cannot be heard of. Out of doubt[1] he is transported.[2]

### FLUTE
If he come not, then the play is marred. It goes not forward,[3]
doth it?

### QUINCE
It is not possible: you have not a man in all Athens able to     5
discharge[4] Pyramus, but he.

### FLUTE
No; he hath simply the best wit of any handicraft man in
Athens.

### QUINCE
Yea, and the best person[5] too; and he is a very paramour[6] for a
sweet voice.     10

### FLUTE
You must say "paragon". A paramour is, God bless us, a thing
of naught.[7]

*Enter* SNUG

### SNUG
Masters! the Duke is coming from the temple, and there is two
or three lords and ladies more married. If our sport had gone
forward,[8] we had all been made men.[9]     15

143

10 *sixpence ... life*, as a reward for his acting. (This was not bad wages for a working man in Shakespeare's time).
11 *could not have scaped* – "could not have failed to get". *scaped*: escaped.
12 *An* – "If".
13 *in Pyramus* – "for acting Pyramus".
14 *or nothing* – "take nothing less".
15 *lads* – "boys"; "friends".
16 *hearts* – "dear friends".
17 *courageous* – "splendid".
18 *right as it fell out* – "just as it happened".

19 *apparel* – "clothes (for the play)".
20 *strings to your beards*, to tie on their false beards.
21 *presently* – "very soon".
22 *the short and the long* – "the whole truth" (the same whether told in short or at length).
23 *preferred* – "chosen". The choice is made in the next scene, but this meeting may be supposed to be going on at the same time as the events at the beginning of v.i.
24 *I do not doubt but* – "I am sure".

### FLUTE

O sweet bully Bottom! Thus hath he lost sixpence a day during his life;[10] he could not have scaped[11] sixpence a day. An[12] the Duke had not given him sixpence a day for playing Pyramus, I 'll be hanged. He would have deserved it: Sixpence a day in Pyramus,[13] or nothing.[14]                                    20

*Enter* BOTTOM

### BOTTOM

Where are these lads?[15] Where are these hearts?[16]

### QUINCE

Bottom! O, most courageous[17] day! O, most happy hour!

### BOTTOM

Masters, I am to discourse wonders; but ask me not what, for if I tell you, I am no true Athenian. I will tell you everything right as it fell out.[18]                                    25

### QUINCE

Let us hear, sweet Bottom.

### BOTTOM

Not a word of me: all that I will tell you is, that the Duke hath dined. Get your apparel[19] together, good strings to your beards,[20] new ribbons to your pumps, meet presently[21] at the palace; every man look o'er his part; for the short and the        30 long[22] is, our play is preferred.[23] In any case, let Thisby have clean linen: and let not him that plays the lion pare his nails, for they shall hang out for the lion's claws. And, most dear actors, eat no onions, nor garlic; for we are to utter sweet breath, and I do not doubt but[24] to hear them say, it is a sweet        35 comedy. No more words: away, go away!

[*Exeunt*

(v.i) At the palace, Theseus and Hippolyta speak of the strange imaginations of lovers, lunatics and poets. The lovers enter and Theseus chooses "Pyramus and Thisby" as the play to be performed at the wedding.

The tragedy of "Pyramus and Thisby", which Hippolyta calls "the silliest stuff that ever I heard", is acted to everybody's amusement. All leave, and Puck enters to sweep the dust from the house.

Oberon and Titania enter the palace with their fairies. They sing, dance, and bless all the newly-married couples and their future children. Puck stays to say good-bye to the audience.

1 *that* – "the story that".

2 *antique* – "ancient"; but the word may be just a different spelling of "*antic*" = strange.

3 *fairy toys* – "idle tales about fairies".

4 *seething brains* – "brains which seem to boil with ideas".

5 *shaping fantasies* – "imaginations (*fantasies*) able to twist reality into strange shapes".

6 *apprehend . . . comprehends* – "take hold of (*apprehend*) more ideas than cool reason can understand (*comprehends*)".

7 *compact* – "composed"; "made up".

8 *Sees Helen's . . . Egypt* – "Sees the most beautiful woman in the world (Helen of Troy) in a woman whose face is as dark as an Egyptian's (*a brow of Egypt*)". He means a *gipsy*. These dark-skinned wandering people of Indian origin were thought to be Egyptians; hence the name "gipsy", short for "Egyptian".

9 *as imagination . . . unknown* – "while the imagination of the poet invents bodies for things of which nothing is known" (such as fairies, elves, etc.).

10 *the poet's pen . . . shapes* – "the poet in his writing describes these as having a definite shape".

11 *and gives to airy nothing . . . name* – "and gives to an imaginary thing (*airy nothing*: a nothing floating in air) a dwelling place (*local habitation*) and a name". (Thus the poet imagines a Fairy Queen, and gives her the forest as a home, with Titania as her name).

12 *if it would . . . of that joy* – "if the imagination wishes to take hold of (*apprehend*) some (idea which gives it) joy, it includes (*comprehends*) an imaginary person bringing the joy". (Thus imagination "apprehends" the idea of love, and "comprehends" with it such a person as Cupid or Venus, bringing love).

*Or . . . a bush supposed a bear.* Working in the same way, the imagination of a man at night forms the idea of fear, and then creates fearful shapes, so that a bush he really sees becomes an imaginary bear.

14 *told over* – "told in detail".

15 *And . . . so together* – "And the fact that the minds of all (the lovers) have undergone such changes (*transfigured so*) together".

# ACT FIVE

*Scene I. Athens.*

*Enter* THESEUS, HIPPOLYTA, PHILOSTRATE *and Attendants.*

HIPPOLYTA

'T is strange, my Theseus, that[1] these lovers speak of.

THESEUS

More strange than true. I never may believe
These antique[2] fables nor these fairy toys.[3]
Lovers and madmen have such seething brains,[4]
Such shaping fantasies,[5] that apprehend                          5
More than cool reason ever comprehends.[6]
The lunatic, the lover, and the poet
Are of imagination all compact.[7]
One sees more devils than vast hell can hold;
That is the madman. The lover, all as frantic,            10
Sees Helen's beauty in a brow of Egypt.[8]
The poet's eye, in a fine frenzy rolling,
Doth glance from heaven to earth, from earth to heaven,
And as imagination bodies forth
The forms of things unknown,[9] the poet's pen            15
Turns them to shapes,[10] and gives to airy nothing
A local habitation and a name.[11]
Such tricks hath strong imagination
That, if it would but apprehend some joy,
It comprehends some bringer of that joy.[12]               20
Or in the night, imagining some fear,
How easy is a bush supposed a bear.[13]

HIPPOLYTA

But all the story of the night told over,[14]
And all their minds transfigured so together,[15]

147

16 *More . . . fancy's images* – "Shows (*witnesseth*) that these are more then mere figures of their imagination (*fancy's images*)".

17 *And grows . . . constancy* – "And amounts to a description in which all the details fit together". *constancy* = "consistency"; a reasonable connection between the parts, which indicates that the account as a whole is true.

18 *howsoever* – "nevertheless"; "all the same".

19 *admirable* – "wonderful".

20 *Accompany your hearts* – "Keep company with your love".

21 *More than to us . . . bed* – "May they (the things you wish us) do even more for you; may they attend you when you walk, when you take your meals (*your board*) and when you sleep (*your bed*)".

22 *after-supper* – "the time after supper".

23 *manager of mirth* – "official who arranges entertainments at court" (known in Shakespeare's time as "Master of the Revels").

24 *To ease . . . hour.* "anguish" and "torturing" give the idea of extreme pain: Theseus uses the words half-jokingly to suggest his impatience for the wedding to be completed.

25 *abridgement* – "way of shortening the time"; "pastime".

26 *beguile the lazy time* – "play a trick on the slow-moving time (to make it pass more quickly)".

27 *brief* – "list".

28 *sports are ripe* – "entertainments are ready to be shown".

*what masques, what dances shall we have*

More witnesseth than fancy's images,[16]       25
And grows to something of great constancy;[17]
But howsoever,[18] strange and admirable.[19]

*Enter* LYSANDER, DEMETRIUS, HERMIA *and* HELENA

### THESEUS
Here come the lovers, full of joy and mirth:
Joy, gentle friends, joy and fresh days of love
Accompany your hearts![20]

### LYSANDER
                  More than to us,    30
Wait in your royal walks, your board, your bed![21]

### THESEUS
Come now, what masques, what dances shall we have
To wear away this long age of three hours
Between our after-supper,[22] and bed-time?
Where is our usual manager of mirth?[23]    35
What revels are in hand? Is there no play
To ease the anguish of a torturing hour?[24]
Call Philostrate.

### PHILOSTRATE
              Here, mighty Theseus.

### THESEUS
Say, what abridgement[25] have you for this evening?
What masque? What music? How shall we beguile    40
The lazy time,[26] if not with some delight?

### PHILOSTRATE
There is a brief[27] how many sports are ripe:[28]
Make choice of which your Highness will see first.

29 *the Centaurs,* imaginary creatures, half horse, half man, against whom Hercules fought.

30 *eunuch,* boy or man with a high voice.

31 *We 'll . . . that* – "We 'll have none of that".

32 *In glory of* – "to show the glory of".

33 *the tipsy Bacchanals* – "the drunken (*tipsy*) worshippers of Bacchus (god of wine)".

34 *the Thracian singer,* Orpheus, the great musician from Thrace (northern Greece), who, according to the ancient stories, was killed in the way described here.

35 *device* – "play or entertainment".

36 *The thrice three Muses,* the nine goddesses who, as the Greeks believed, gave men the urge to different kinds of musical and poetic composition.

37 *Learning . . . beggary* – "Learning, who recently died as poor as a beggar". The play would be about learned men who died poor and neglected. Shakespeare's rival dramatist, Greene, died in this state, and the words may refer to him.

38 *sorting with* – "agreeing with".

39 *hot ice . . . snow.* The words describing the play disagree with each other as much as "hot ice" and snow in that strange state of being warm.

40 *the concord . . . discord* – "the agreement in this disagreement".

41 *fitted* – "suitable".

42 *it,* i.e. the play about Pyramus, not the "ten word play", which is only mentioned to show how a play can be both "brief" and "tedious".

43 *confess* – "admit".

44 *Made mine eyes water* – "Made tears come" (but tears caused by laughter, not sorrow).

150

THESEUS (*reads*)

"The battle with the Centaurs,[29] to be sung
By an Athenian eunuch,[30] to the harp".                          45
We 'll none[31] of that. That have I told my love
In glory of[32] my kinsman Hercules.
"The riot of the tipsy Bacchanals,[33]
Tearing the Thracian singer[34] in their rage".
That is an old device,[35] and it was played                      50
When I from Thebes came last a conqueror.
"The thrice three Muses,[36] mourning for the death
Of Learning, late deceased in beggary".[37]
That is some satire, keen and critical,
Not sorting with[38] a nuptial ceremony.                          55
"A tedious brief scene of young Pyramus
And his love Thisby; very tragical mirth".
Merry and tragical? Tedious, and brief?
That is, hot ice, and wondrous strange snow.[39]
How shall we find the concord of this discord?[40]               60

PHILOSTRATE

A play there is, my lord, some ten words long,
Which is as brief as I have known a play;
But by ten words, my lord, it is too long,
Which makes it tedious; for in all the play
There is not one word apt, one player fitted.[41]                65
And tragical, my noble lord, it[42] is;
For Pyramus therein doth kill himself.
Which when I saw rehearsed, I must confess,[43]
Made mine eyes water;[44] but more merry tears,
The passion of loud laughter never shed.                         70

THESEUS

What are they that do play it?

PHILOSTRATE

Hard-handed men, that work in Athens here,

151

45 *in* – "with".

46 *toiled . . . memories* – "put their unpractised (*unbreathed*) memories to work (in learning their parts)".

47 *against* – "in preparation for".

48 *Extremely stretched* – "Over-exercised".

49 *conned . . . pain* – "learned by heart with much suffering".

50 *wretchedness o'ercharged* – "too heavy a burden laid on poor men".

51 *duty . . . perishing* – "men suffering while trying to do their duty".

52 *in this kind* – "in this style"; i.e. in acting.

53 *Our sport . . . mistake* – "Our pleasure will be in taking their mistakes as correct" (with word-play on *take* and *mistake*).

*Centaurs* [29]

152

Which never laboured in[45] their minds till now;
And now have toiled their unbreathed memories[46]
With this same play, against[47] your nuptial.                    75

THESEUS

And we will hear it.

PHILOSTRATE

                No, my noble lord,
It is not for you. I have heard it over,
And it is nothing, nothing in the world;
Unless you can find sport in their intents,
Extremely stretched[48] and conned with cruel pain,[49]        80
To do you service.

THESEUS

                I will hear that play.
For never any thing can be amiss
When simpleness and duty tender it.
Go, bring them in; and take your places, ladies.

                    [*Exit* PHILOSTRATE

HIPPOLYTA

I love not to see wretchedness o'ercharged,[50]                  85
And duty in his service perishing.[51]

THESEUS

Why, gentle sweet, you shall see no such thing.

HIPPOLYTA

He says they can do nothing in this kind.[52]

THESEUS

The kinder we, to give them thanks for nothing.
Our sport shall be to take what they mistake;[53]                90

54 *noble respect* – "the noble way of seeing things".

55 *Takes it in might, not merit* – "Accepts it for the effort made (*in might*), not the merit".

56 *clerks* – "men of learning".

57 *purposéd* – "made it their purpose"; "intended".

58 *periods* – "full stops" (they have stopped in the middle of the sentences in their prepared speeches – just as Quince will do).

59 *Throttle . . . fears* – "In their fear, swallow down (*Throttle*) the words (*accent*) they had practised to speak".

60 *dumbly . . . off* – "stopped in the middle as if dumb".

61 *read* – "understood".

62 *rattling tongue* – "rapid, easy talk".

63 *saucy and audacious eloquence* – "cheeky and over-daring persons, with practice in speech-making (*eloquence*)".

64 *tongue-tied* – "unable to speak freely".

65 *to my capacity* – "as far as I can understand".

66 *the Prologue* – "the actor who is to speak the prologue".

67 *addressed* – "ready".

Lines 109–118: Quince gets all the stops in this speech mixed up, so that the meaning sounds quite different from what was intended. For example, lines 115–16 should read:

Our true intent is all for your delight.
We are not here that you should here repent you.

68 *the true . . . end* – "our true purpose".

69 *in despite* – "with bad intentions".

70 *minding* – "intending".

71 *repent you* – "regret (seeing the play)".

154

And what poor duty cannot do, noble respect[54]
Takes it in might, not merit.[55]
Where I have come, great clerks[56] have purposéd[57]
To greet me with premeditated welcomes;
Where I have seen them shiver and look pale,                    95
Make periods[58] in the midst of sentences,
Throttle their practised accent in their fears,[59]
And in conclusion, dumbly have broken off,[60]
Not paying me a welcome. Trust me, sweet,
Out of this silence yet I picked a welcome;                    100
And in the modesty of fearful duty
I read[61] as much as from the rattling tongue[62]
Of saucy and audacious eloquence.[63]
Love, therefore, and tongue-tied[64] simplicity,
In least speak most, to my capacity.[65]                       105

*Re-enter* PHILOSTRATE

PHILOSTRATE
So please your Grace, the Prologue[66] is addressed.[67]

THESEUS
Let him approach.

*Trumpets sound*
*Enter* QUINCE *as the* PROLOGUE

QUINCE (*as* PROLOGUE)
If we offend, it is with our good will.
That you should think, we come not to offend,
But with good will. To show our simple skill,                  110
That is the true beginning of our end.[68]
Consider then, we come but in despite.[69]
We do not come, as minding[70] to content you,
Our true intent is. All for your delight,
We are not here. That you should here repent you,[71]           115

155

72 *like* – "likely".

73 *stand upon points* – "worry about small matters" (with word-play – "does not stop at the points" in a sentence).

74 *rid* – "ridden" (as one rides a horse).

75 *he knows not the stop* – "he does not know how to stop" (the same joke).

76 *good moral* – "good lesson in behaviour".

77 *speak true* – "speak correctly".

78 *in government* – "in control (of the stops of the recorder)".

79 *nothing . . . disordered* – "nothing damaged but all out of order" (like links in the chain, all the words were there; but because of the wrong stops, the sense was confused).

80 *Gentles* – "Ladies and gentlemen".

81 *perchance* – "perhaps".

82 *think no scorn* – "not think it shameful".

The actors are at hand: and by their show,
You shall know all, that you are like[72] to know.

#### THESEUS

This fellow doth not stand upon points.[73]

#### LYSANDER

He hath rid[74] his prologue like a rough colt: he knows not the
stop.[75] A good moral,[76] my lord: it is not enough to speak, but    120
to speak true.[77]

#### HIPPOLYTA

Indeed he hath played on his prologue like a child on a
recorder, a sound, but not in government.[78]

#### THESEUS

His speech was like a tangled chain: nothing impaired, but all
disordered.[79] Who is next?    125

*A trumpet sounds. Enter* PYRAMUS (BOTTOM), THISBE
(FLUTE), WALL (SNOUT), MOONSHINE (STARVELING), *and*
LION (SNUG), *who stand in line while* QUINCE *speaks as*
PROLOGUE

#### QUINCE (*as* PROLOGUE)

Gentles,[80] perchance[81] you wonder at this show;
But wonder on, till truth make all things plain.
This man is Pyramus, if you would know;
This beauteous lady Thisby is certain.
This man with lime and rough-cast doth present    130
Wall, that vile Wall, which did these lovers sunder:
And through Wall's chink, poor souls, they are content
To whisper: at the which, let no man wonder.
This man, with lantern, dog, and bush of thorn,
Presenteth Moonshine; for, if you will know,    135
By moonshine did these lovers think no scorn[82]

157

83 *grisly* – "fearful to see".
84 *hight* – "is called".
85 *trusty* – "true".
86 *affright* – "frighten".
87 *fall* – "let fall".
88 *tall* – "fine"; "good-looking".
89 *broached* – "pierced".
90 *boiling bloody breast.* This line, together with the one before it, has nine words beginning with "b". Shakespeare is making fun of the old-fashioned tragic plays which made much use of this artificial style in passionate speeches.

91 *tarrying in mulberry shade* – "waiting in the shade of a mulberry tree".
92 *twain* – "two" (Pyramus and Thisbe).
93 *At large discourse* – "Speak (*discourse*) at length".
94 *interlude* – (see glossary and I.ii.5).
95 *sinister* – "left". (Snout here puts the fingers of his right and left hands together to make the "cranny").

158

To meet at Ninus' tomb, there, there to woo.
This grisly[83] beast, which Lion hight[84] by name,
The trusty[85] Thisby, coming first by night,
Did scare away, or rather did affright:[86]                    140
And as she fled, her mantle she did fall;[87]
Which Lion vile with bloody mouth did stain.
Anon comes Pyramus, sweet youth and tall,[88]
And finds his trusty Thisby's mantle slain;
Whereat with blade, with bloody blameful blade,              145
He bravely broached[89] his boiling bloody breast,[90]
And Thisby, tarrying in mulberry shade,[91]
His dagger drew, and died. For all the rest,
Let Lion, Moonshine, Wall, and Lovers twain,[92]
At large discourse,[93] while here they do remain.           150

*[Exeunt all the players but* SNOUT (WALL)

THESEUS

I wonder if the lion be to speak.

DEMETRIUS

No wonder, my lord: one lion may, when many asses do.

SNOUT (*as* WALL)

In this same interlude[94] it doth befall
That I, one Snout by name, present a wall:
And such a wall, as I would have you think,                  155
That had in it a crannied hole or chink,
Through which the lovers, Pyramus and Thisby,
Did whisper often, very secretly.
This loam, this rough-cast, and this stone doth show
That I am that same Wall; the truth is so.                   160
And this the cranny is, right and sinister,[95]
Through which the fearful lovers are to whisper.

THESEUS

Would you desire lime and hair to speak better?

159

96 *partition* – "dividing wall".

97 *draws near* – "approaches".

98 *grim-looked* – "grim-looking".

99 *art* – "are".

100 *alack*, expression of regret, like "alas".

101 *blink through* – "peep through".

102 *eyne* (rhymes with "mine") "eyes".

103 *Jove shield* – *Jove*: king and greatest of the gods in the ancient religion (called "Zeus" by the Greeks). *shield*: protect.

104 *being sensible* – "having feelings of its own" (since "Wall" is acted by a man).

105 *again* – "back" (at Pyramus, for cursing its stones).

106 *spy* – "espy"; "catch sight of".

107 *pat* – "just".

#### DEMETRIUS

It is the wittiest partition[96] that ever I heard discourse, my lord.

#### THESEUS

Pyramus draws near[97] the Wall; silence.                    165

*Enter* BOTTOM *as* PYRAMUS

#### BOTTOM (*as* PYRAMUS)

O grim-looked[98] night, O night with hue so black!
O night, which ever art[99] when day is not!
O night, O night; alack,[100] alack, alack,
I fear my Thisby's promise is forgot.
And thou O wall, O sweet, O lovely wall,                    170
That stand'st between her father's ground and mine,
Thou wall, O wall, O sweet and lovely wall,
Show me thy chink, to blink through[101] with mine eyne.[102]

[SNOUT *holds up his fingers*

Thanks, courteous wall: Jove shield[103] thee well for this!
But what see I? No Thisby do I see.                         175
O wicked wall, through whom I see no bliss,
Cursed be thy stones for thus deceiving me!

#### THESEUS

The wall, methinks, being sensible,[104] should curse again.[105]

#### BOTTOM (*as* PYRAMUS)

No in truth sir, he should not. "Deceiving me" is Thisby's cue;
she is to enter now, and I am to spy[106] her through the wall. 180
You shall see it will fall pat[107] as I told you: yonder she comes.

*Enter* FLUTE (*as* THISBE)

#### FLUTE (*as* THISBE)

O wall, full often hast thou heard my moans,

108 *cherry lips* – "lips as red as cherries" (as in III.ii.140).
109 *knit up* – "bound together".
110 *an* – "if".
111 *thy lover's grace* – "thy true lover".
112 *Limander*. He means Leander, the Greek lover who was drowned while swimming across the Hellespont (between Europe and Asia) to meet Hero, his beloved.
113 *Helen*. "Thisbe" means to say Hero.
114 *the Fates*, three Greek goddesses who decided all the events in a man's life – hence our word "Fate" (q.v.).

115 *Shafalus, Procrus,* meaning Cephalus and Procris, another loving pair in Greek stories. Cephalus, rather like Pyramus, was by mistake the cause of his wife's death.
116 *Ninny's* – see note 36 to III.i.
117 *'Tide life, 'tide death* – "whether life or death results". *tide* = "betide", q.v.

For parting my fair Pyramus and me.
My cherry lips[108] have often kissed thy stones;
Thy stones, with lime and hair knit up[109] in thee.                    185

BOTTOM (*as* PYRAMUS)
I see a voice; now will I to the chink,
To spy an[110] I can hear my Thisby's face.
Thisby!
                    FLUTE (*as* THISBE)
My love! thou art my love, I think.

BOTTOM (*as* PYRAMUS)
Think what thou wilt, I am thy lover's grace,[111]                    190
And like Limander[112] am I trusty still.

FLUTE (*as* THISBE)
And I like Helen,[113] till the Fates[114] me kill.

BOTTOM (*as* PYRAMUS)
Not Shafalus to Procrus[115] was so true.

FLUTE (*as* THISBE)
As Shafalus to Procrus, I to you.

BOTTOM (*as* PYRAMUS)
O kiss me through the hole of this vile wall.                    195

FLUTE (*as* THISBE)
I kiss the wall's hole, not your lips at all.

BOTTOM (*as* PYRAMUS)
Wilt thou at Ninny's[116] tomb meet me straightway?

FLUTE (*as* THISBE)
'Tide life, 'tide death,[117] I come without delay.
                    [*Exeunt* BOTTOM *and* FLUTE
163

118 *Now is the moon used.* Since the actor playing "Wall" has gone off, Theseus expects that the players will have to use "Moon" instead. (Some editions print "Now is the mural (= wall) down"; but this is less likely to be what Shakespeare wrote).

119 *No remedy* – "It can't be helped"; "There's no other way".

120 *The best . . . kind* – "The best actors".

121 *shadows* – "mere imitations of men".

122 *if . . . them* – "if we make them better with our imagination".

123 *if we imagine . . . themselves* – "if we have as good an opinion of them as they have of themselves".

124 *I, one Snug the joiner am . . . dam* – "it is I, Snug the joiner, who am a cruel (*fell*) lion; for surely I am not a lioness (*lion's dam*)".

SNOUT (*as* WALL)

Thus have I, Wall, my part dischargéd so;
And being done, thus Wall away doth go.          [*Exit* 200

THESEUS

Now is the Moon used[118] between the two neighbours.

DEMETRIUS

No remedy,[119] my lord, when walls are so wilful, to hear
without warning.

HIPPOLYTA

This is the silliest stuff that ever I heard.

THESEUS

The best in this kind[120] are but shadows,[121] and the worst are no 205
worse, if imagination amend them.[122]

HIPPOLYTA

It must be your imagination then, and not theirs.

THESEUS

If we imagine no worse of them than they of themselves,[123]
they may pass for excellent men. Here come two noble beasts
in, a man and a lion.                                              210

*Enter* SNUG *as* LION *and* STARVELING *as* MOONSHINE

SNUG (*as* LION)

You, ladies, you, whose gentle hearts do fear
The smallest monstrous mouse that creeps on floor,
May now, perchance, both quake and tremble here
When Lion rough in wildest rage doth roar.
Then know that I, one Snug the joiner, am                          215
A lion fell, nor else no lion's dam:[124]

165

125 *'t were pity . . . life*, the words Bottom wished to be said (III.i.34).

126 *of a good conscience* – "with a true feeling for others".

127 *a very fox for his valour* – "like a fox for courage"; the fox being well-known as a cowardly animal.

128 *a goose for his discretion* – "like a goose for caution"; the goose being regarded as a foolish bird.

129 *his valour . . . goose.* The joke is a kind of clever game which turns upon word-play, since "carry', also meant "be greater than". Snug the Lion, it has been said, has the "valour" of a fox, and the "discretion" of a goose. Since the fox carries the goose, answers Demetrius, his valour "carries" (is greater than) his discretion. But Snug's valour is certainly *not* greater; therefore he cannot be as described.

130 *His discretion . . . the fox.* But, Theseus replies, since a goose does not carry a fox, his discretion cannot "carry" (be greater than) his valour.

131 *leave . . . discretion* – "leave it for him to decide (whether he is a fox or a goose)".

132 *This lanthorn . . . present* – "This lantern represents the moon with its horns (i.e. the pointed tips of the moon when it is not full)". "Horned" is suggested by the old spelling "*lanthorn*" — lantern made of horn (pronounced "lant-horn").

133 *the horns on his head*, believed to be the sign of a man whose wife deceives him.

134 *no crescent – crescent:* the shape of the moon while it is still growing to fullness.

135 *within the circumference* – "inside the circular cover (of the lantern)".

136 *the man i' th' moon.* Seen from Europe, the dark spots on the moon give it the look of a man's face; this imaginary face was called "the man in the moon".

*This lanthorn doth the hornéd moon present*

For if I should as Lion come in strife
Into this place, 't were pity on my life.[125]

THESEUS

A very gentle beast, and of a good conscience.[126]

DEMETRIUS

The very best at a beast, my lord, that e'er I saw.                    220

LYSANDER

This Lion is a very fox for his valour.[127]

THESEUS

True, and a goose for his discretion.[128]

DEMETRIUS

Not so, my lord; for his valour cannot carry his discretion, and
the fox carries the goose.[129]

THESEUS

His discretion, I am sure, cannot carry his valour; for the goose 225
carries not the fox.[130] It is well; leave it to his discretion,[131]
and let us listen to the Moon.

STARVELING (*as* MOONSHINE)

This lanthorn doth the hornéd moon present.[132]

DEMETRIUS

He should have worn the horns on his head.[133]

THESEUS

He is no crescent[134] and his horns are invisible, within the cir- 230
cumference.[135]

STARVELING (*as* MOONSHINE)

This lanthorn doth the hornéd moon present:
Myself the Man i' th' Moon[136] do seem to be.

167

137 *the man . . . lantern.* If "Moon-shine" is the man in the moon, and the lantern is the moon, then he should be inside his own lantern.

138 *in snuff* – "smoking".

139 *would he would change* – "I wish he would change as the moon does".

140 *by his . . . discretion* – "by his (i.e., his lantern's) low, cautious light" (but "by one's light of discretion" also means "by such wisdom as one has"; so "his small light" means "his small amount of wisdom").

141 *stay the time* – "wait out the time (until the play ends)".

142 *this thorn-bush . . . dog* – supposed to belong to "the man in the moon".

**THESEUS**

This is the greatest error of all the rest; the man should be put
Into the lantern.[137] How is it else the Man i' th' Moon? 235

**DEMETRIUS**

He dares not come there for the candle; for you see, it is already
in snuff.[138]

**HIPPOLYTA**

I am a-weary of this Moon; would he would change![139]

**THESEUS**

It appears, by his small light of discretion,[140] that he is in the
wane: but yet, in courtesy, in all reason, we must stay the 240
time.[141]

**LYSANDER**

Proceed, Moon.

**STARVELING** (*as* MOONSHINE)

All that I have to say is to tell you that the lantern is the Moon;
I, the Man i' th' Moon; this thornbush, my thorn-bush; and
this dog, my dog.[142] 245

**DEMETRIUS**

Why, all these should be in the lantern: for all these are in the
Moon. But silence, here comes Thisby.

*Re-enter* FLUTE (*as* THISBE)

**FLUTE** (*as* THISBE)

This is old Ninny's tomb. Where is my love?

**SNUG** (*as* LION) *roars*

Oh-h-h-!                                             [THISBE *runs off*

**DEMETRIUS**

Well roared, Lion. 250

G                                    169

143 *with a good grace* – "with much
pleasure".
144 *well moused.* "Lion" has pawed at
Thisbe's mantle like a cat catching
a mouse. *to mouse:* to catch a
mouse.
145 *I trust* – "I hope".
146 *to take . . . sight* – "to have sight of
truest Thisby".
147 *dreadful dole* – "fearful sorrow".
148 *dainty duck* – rather like "dear
darling".
149 *Furies,* spirits of anger and punishment in the ancient Greek religion,
and in Roman plays, whose style
old-fashioned Elizabethan plays
used to copy. So with "Fates" in
the next line.

150 *Cut thread and thrum* – "Cut all the
threads which tie my life together". *Thrum:* a kind of thread
used in weaving; which reminds
the audience that Bottom the
weaver is speaking.
151 *Quail, crush, conclude and quell.*
This piling up of "c" sounds has
the same effect as the "b" sounds
in lines 145-6 above (see note 90).
Notice also "gracious, golden,
glittering gleams" earlier in this
speech, to make the lines more
"tragic".

**THESEUS**

Well run, Thisby.

**HIPPOLYTA**

Well shone, Moon.
Truly, the Moon shines with a good grace.[143]

[SNUG (*as* LION) *tears* THISBE'S *mantle, and exit*

**THESEUS**

Well moused,[144] Lion.

*Re-enter* BOTTOM (*as* PYRAMUS)

**DEMETRIUS**

And then came Pyramus.                                       255

**LYSANDER**

And so the Lion vanished.

**BOTTOM** (*as* PYRAMUS)

Sweet Moon, I thank thee for thy sunny beams;
I thank thee, Moon, for shining now so bright;
For by thy gracious, golden, glittering gleams,
I trust[145] to take of truest Thisby sight.[146]                260
But stay! O spite!
But mark, poor knight,
What dreadful dole[147] is here!
Eyes, do you see?
How can it be?                                               265
O dainty duck![148] O dear!
Thy mantle good,
What, stained with blood?
Approach, ye Furies[149] fell:
O Fates! come, come:                                         270
Cut thread and thrum,[150]
Quail, crush, conclude, and quell![151]

171

152 *This passion . . . look sad.* The "passion" of Pyramus would then, of course, make no difference. An old saying rather like this was: "He who loses his wife and sixpence, has lost sixpence".

153 *Beshrew . . . I –* "may I be accursed if I do not". *beshrew :* to curse.

154 *frame –* "create".

155 *deflowered –* "taken the flower of life from".

156 *with cheer –* "with kindness". Notice the "l"s in this line.

157 *confound –* "throw into confusion".

158 *pap –* "point of the breast".

159 *hop –* "beat".

160 *No die . . . but one.* Demetrius plays on the word "die" (q.v.). Bottom is not a die – which may have any number on it up to six; he is an ace at cards, with one mark only; "for he is but one", there is nobody like him.

161 *prove –* "show himself to be".

#### THESEUS

This passion, and the death of a dear friend, would go near to
make a man look sad.¹⁵²

#### HIPPOLYTA

Beshrew my heart, but I¹⁵³ pity the man.                    275

#### BOTTOM (*as* PYRAMUS)

O wherefore, Nature, didst thou lions frame?¹⁵⁴
Since lion vile hath here deflowered¹⁵⁵ my dear:
Which is – no, no, which was – the fairest Dame
That lived, that loved, that liked, that looked with cheer.¹⁵⁶
Come tears, confound:¹⁵⁷                                    280
Out sword, and wound
The pap¹⁵⁸ of Pyramus:
Ay, that left pap,
Where heart doth hop;¹⁵⁹
Thus die I, thus, thus, thus.                              285
                                        [*Stabs himself*

Now am I dead,
Now am I fled,
My soul is in the sky,
Tongue, lose thy light,
Moon, take thy flight,                                     290
                [*Exit* STARVELING *as* MOONSHINE
Now die, die, die, die, die.                    [*"Dies"*

#### DEMETRIUS

No die, but an ace for him; for he is but one.¹⁶⁰

#### LYSANDER

Less than an ace, man; for he is dead, he is nothing.

#### THESEUS

With the help of a surgeon he might yet recover, and prove¹⁶¹
an ass.                                                    295

162 *How chance* – "how does it happen".

163 *a long one* – "a long passion" (i.e. a long "tragic" speech).

164 *A mote . . . the better* – "If we were to weigh Pyramus and Thisby on a pair of scales, a grain of dust (*mote*) would turn the scale (*balance*) as to which is the better actor, Pyramus or Thisby" (since they are equally bad).

165 *God warrant us* – "God preserve us".

166 *videlicet* – "namely" (Latin).

167 *These lily lips, this cherry nose.* "Thisby" gets her colours confused; the lily being the model of whiteness, the cherry of redness.

#### HIPPOLYTA

How chance[162] Moonshine is gone before Thisby comes back,
and finds her lover?

*Re-enter* FLUTE (*as* THISBE)

#### THESEUS

She will find him by starlight. Here she comes, and her passion
ends the play.

#### HIPPOLYTA

Methinks she should not use a long one[163] for such a Pyramus; 300
I hope she will be brief.

#### DEMETRIUS

A mote will turn the balance, which Pyramus, which Thisby is
the better;[164] he for a man, God warrant us,[165] she for a
woman, God bless us.

#### LYSANDER

She hath spied him already with those sweet eyes.                    305

#### DEMETRIUS

And she moans, *videlicet*:[166]

#### FLUTE (*as* THISBE)

Asleep, my love?
What, dead, my dove?
O Pyramus, arise!
Speak, speak. Quite dumb?                                            310
Dead, dead? A tomb
Must cover thy sweet eyes.
These lily lips,
This cherry nose,[167]
These yellow cowslip cheeks,                                         315

175

168 *Sisters three*, the three Fates (see note 114).

169 *shore* – (= sheared) "cut in two".

170 *his thread* – "the thread of his (Pyramus's) life". So Pyramus in line 217 calls on the Fates to "cut thread and thrum".

171 *to see . . . to hear*. The epilogue should be "heard", or the dance "seen".

172 *Bergomask dance*, a rough, simple country dance.

173 *Marry* – See note 8 to I.ii.

174 *if he that . . . tragedy*. Theseus thinks it would have been a better play if the author (*he that writ it*) had hanged himself in it.

175 *discharged:* "performed".

Are gone, are gone:
Lovers, make moan:
His eyes were green as leeks.
O Sisters Three,[168]
Come, come to me,                                                    320
With hands as pale as milk;
Lay them in gore,
Since you have shore[169]
With shears his thread[170] of silk.
Tongue, not a word:                                                  325
Come, trusty sword:
Come blade, my breast imbrue:

                                                    [*Stabs herself*

And farewell, friends;
Thus Thisby ends;
Adieu, adieu, adieu.                                                 330

                                                    [*"Dies"*

#### THESEUS
Moonshine and Lion are left to bury the dead.

#### DEMETRIUS
Ay, and Wall too.

#### BOTTOM (*getting up*)
No, I assure you, the wall is down that parted their fathers.
Will it please you to see the epilogue, or to hear[171] a Bergo-
mask dance[172] between two of our company?                          335

#### THESEUS
No epilogue, I pray you; for your play needs no excuse. Never
excuse; for when the players are all dead there need none to be
blamed. Marry,[173] if he that writ it had played Pyramus, and
hanged himself in Thisby's garter, it would have been a fine
tragedy:[174] and so it is truly, and very notably discharged.[175]  340
But come, your Bergomask: let your epilogue alone.

H                                  177

176 *The iron . . . twelve* – "The iron clapper of the bell (*tongue*) has sounded twelve times for midnight".

177 *fairy time* – "the time when the fairies come out" (According to Oberon, III.ii. 388–93, they stay out until the sun has risen).

178 *out-sleep the coming morn . . . over-watched* – "sleep as late tomorrow morning as we have stayed up late (*overwatched*) tonight".

179 *palpable gross* – "coarse and heavy".

180 *beguiled . . . night* – "deceived the heavily-moving night", i.e. kept back the advance of night.

181 *solemnity* – "rejoicing" (See IV.i.84, 130, notes 45 and 80).

182 *behowls* – "howls at" (some editions print *beholds* = "looks at").

183 *heavy* – "heavily sleeping".

184 *fordone* – "tired out".

185 *the wasted . . . glow* – "the logs of wood in the fire (*brands*), nearly burnt out (*wasted*), shine with a dull light (*glow*)".

186 *Puts the wretch . . . shroud* – "Makes the poor man (*wretch*), lying in pain, think of a shroud (i.e. of his approaching death)". It was believed that the cry of an owl foretold a death.

187 *Every one . . . sprite* – "Every grave lets out the spirit of the dead".

188 *run . . . Hecate's team* – "follow the triple Hecate" (pronounced "Heckat"). She was the goddess of darkness and magic, and was called "triple" because the ancient statues and pictures showed her as three forms in one.

189 *frolic* – "cheerful".

190 *not a mouse*, i.e. not the least little thing.

191 *hallowed* – "made holy" (by the marriages conducted).

192 *To sweep . . . door.* The dust collected behind the great main doors of the hall, which in the old country houses nearly always stood open. Puck in sweeping this away will show himself an excellent servant to Theseus and Hippolyta.

178

*A Bergomask dance*

The iron tongue of midnight hath told twelve.[176]
Lovers, to bed; 't is almost fairy time.[177]
I fear we shall out-sleep the coming morn
As much as we this night have overwatched.[178]                        345
This palpable gross[179] play hath well beguiled
The heavy gait of night.[180] Sweet friends, to bed.
A fortnight hold we this solemnity,[181]
In nightly revels and new jollity.

[*Exeunt all*

*Enter* PUCK *with a broom*

PUCK

Now the hungry lion roars,                                             350
And the wolf behowls[182] the moon;
Whilst the heavy[183] ploughman snores,
All with weary task fordone.[184]
Now the wasted brands do glow,[185]
Whilst the screech-owl, screeching loud,                               355
Puts the wretch that lies in woe
In remembrance of a shroud.[186]
Now it is the time of night
That the graves, all gaping wide,
Every one lets forth his sprite,[187]                                  360
In the church-way paths to glide.
And we fairies, that do run
By the triple Hecate's team[188]
From the presence of the sun,
Following darkness like a dream,                                       365
Now are frolic;[189] not a mouse[190]
Shall disturb this hallowed[191] house.
I am sent with broom before,
To sweep the dust behind the door.[192]

*Enter* OBERON *and* TITANIA, *the King and Queen of Fairies, with
their train, bearing lighted candles*

179

193 *trippingly* – "with a light tread".

194 *rehearse . . . rote* – "repeat (*rehearse*) your song from memory".

195 *To each word . . . note* – "Sing each word with a gentle, continuous musical sound (*warbling note*)". In this style of singing the words could not be heard through the "warble"; hence no words are given for the fairies' song.

196 *break of day* – "first light of day".

197 *stray* – "roam about".

198 *the best bride-bed* – "the best bed of those newly married", i.e. that of Theseus and Hippolyta.

199 *create* – "created".

200 *the blots . . . hand* – "the faults made by Nature".

201 *stand* – "be present".

202 *mark prodigious* – "mark considered unlucky" (such as the birthmarks mentioned in the line before).

203 *Despiséd in nativity* – "Regarded with dislike when found on a newborn child (*in nativity*)'.

204 *field-dew consecrate* – "dew taken from the fields and blessed by the fairies".

205 *take his gait* – "make his way".

206 *several* – "particular".

*Enter* OBERON *and* TITANIA, *the King and Queen of Fairies, with their train, bearing lighted candles*

### OBERON

Through the house give glimmering light, 370
By the dead and drowsy fire;
Every elf and fairy sprite
Hop as light as bird from brier;
And this ditty after me
Sing, and dance it trippingly.[193] 375

### TITANIA

First rehearse your song by rote,[194]
To each word a warbling note.[195]
Hand in hand, with fairy grace,
Will we sing and bless this place.

OBERON *leads, and the Fairies sing and dance*

### OBERON

Now until the break of day,[196] 380
Through this house each fairy stray.[197]
To the best bride-bed[198] will we,
Which by us shall blessèd be;
And the issue there create[199]
Ever shall be fortunate. 385
So shall all the couples three
Ever true in loving be;
And the blots of Nature's hand[200]
Shall not in their issue stand.[201]
Never mole, hare-lip, nor scar, 390
Nor mark prodigious,[202] such as are
Despisèd in nativity,[203]
Shall upon their children be.
With this field-dew consecrate,[204]
Every fairy take his gait,[205] 395
And each several[206] chamber bless,
Through this palace, with sweet peace;
And the owner of it blest

181

207 *we shadows* – "we actors" (Theseus also described actors as "shadows"; see notes 120, 121).

208 *all is mended* – "all is set right".

209 *idle theme* – "unimportant story".

210 *No more . . . dream* – "Providing nothing but a dream to think about".

211 *we will mend* – "we will improve".

212 *as I am* – "as true as I am".

213 *unearnéd luck* – "good luck that we have not deserved".

214 *to 'scape . . . tongue* – "to escape ('scape) from the noise a snake makes (*serpent's tongue*)", i.e. hissing. Elizabethan audiences would hiss the actors in a bad play.

215 *make amends ere long* – "put things right soon" (by putting on another and better play).

216 *Give me your hands* – "Clap your hands for me" (to show you liked the play).

217 *Robin . . . amends* – "Robin Goodfellow, i.e. Puck, will make things right" (as promised four lines before).

Ever shall in safety rest.
Trip away, make no stay;                                          400
Meet me all by break of day.

> [*Exeunt,* OBERON *and* TITANIA *behind, the Fairies*
> *through the house.* PUCK *stays*

PUCK

If we shadows[207] have offended,
Think but this, and all is mended,[208]
That you have but slumbered here,
While these visions did appear.                                  405
And this weak and idle theme,[209]
No more yielding but a dream,[210]
Gentles, do not reprehend:
If you pardon, we will mend.[211]
And, as I am[212] an honest Puck,                                410
If we have unearnéd luck[213]
Now to scape the serpent's tongue,[214]
We will make amends ere long;[215]
Else the Puck a liar call.
So, good night unto you all.                                     415
Give me your hands,[216] if we be friends,
And Robin shall restore amends.[217]

> [*Exit*

Ever shall in safety rest,
... shall ... make no stop,
Meet me all by break of day.

[*Exeunt* OBERON, TITANIA, PUCK, *the Fairy*]
... ... part of the house, PUCK *only*

*Puck.* If we shadows have offended,                                    410
Think but this, and all is mended,
That you have but slumbered here,
While these visions did appear.
And this weak and idle theme,
No more yielding but a dream,
Gentles, do not reprehend:
If you pardon, we will mend.
And, as I am an honest Puck,
If we have unearned luck
Now to scape the serpent's tongue,
We will make amends ere long;                                          420
Else the Puck a liar call:
So, good night unto you all.
Give me your hands, if we be friends,
And Robin shall restore amends.

# GLOSSARY

This glossary explains all those words in the play which are used in Modern English as they were in Shakespeare's day, but are not among the 3,000 most-used words in the language.

The notes opposite the text explain words which are *not* used in Modern English. In these notes it has been necessary to use a very few words which are also outside the 3,000-word list; these are included in the glossary.

Explanations in the glossary are given entirely within the chosen list of words, except in a few cases where a word is followed by *q.v.*, meaning "see this (word)"; this shows that the word used will itself be found explained elsewhere in the glossary.

Only the meaning of the word as used in the text or notes is normally given.

n. = "noun"; v. = "verb".

## A

*abjure*, swear to give up.
*abound*, be abundant, plentiful.
*acorn*, fruit of the oak (q.v.), which grows in a small natural cup. (Used in III.ii.334 to describe a very small person.)
*adder*, small poisonous snake.
*adieu*, good-bye (French).
*affright*, frighten.
*alas*, an expression of grief or regret.
*ale*, light-coloured beer.
*almanac* (see *calendar*).
*amen*, may it be so (Hebrew, from the Bible): said at the end of a prayer.
*amend* (make amends), to set right.
*amiable*, lovable.
*amiss*, out of order.
*amity*, friendship
*amorous*, desiring love.
*anoint*, put liquid upon the head, for religious or magic purposes.

*ape*, kind of monkey without a tail.
*apprehend*, *apprehension*, power to take in an experience through the senses of the mind (as distinct from *comprehension*, ability to relate it to other things known).
*apricot* (Elizabethan spelling: *apricock*), small orange-coloured fruit with stone in it, rather like a plum.
*apt*, fitting.
*archery*, the use of bow and arrows.
*ass*, donkey.
*astray*, out of the right way.
*attendant*, follower or servant.
*audacious*, daring.
*aught*, anything.
*austerity*, rough, simple way of living.

## B

*bachelor*, an unmarried man.
*bait* (v.), annoy.

*ballad,* a story told in verse to be spoken or sung in public.

*bank* (n.), piece of raised, sloping ground.

*bankrupt* (n.), person who is unable to pay his debts.

*bark* (n.), outer covering or "skin" of trees.

*barren,* (1) not able to bear children; (2) lacking in ideas.

*bashfulness,* feeling of shame or awkwardness in a maiden or child.

*bat,* a small mouse-like animal that flies by night.

*bear* (n.), heavy wild animal with thick brown or black fur.

*bee,* a large, stinging insect which makes honey (q.v.).

*beetle,* kind of insect with hard, shiny wing-cases.

*befall,* happen (to).

*beguile,* deceive.

*behold,* look upon.

*bellows,* instrument for blowing air into a fire (or here, into the pipes of an organ).

*belly,* middle of the body; *bellied,* belly-shaped.

*beloved,* loved.

*bequeath* (v.), give a present.

*beseech,* beg (someone) for (something); *beseech your name,* "beg to know your name".

*betide,* happen, result (v.).

*betrothed,* engaged to be married ("one who has given his *troth*" = pledge).

*betwixt,* between.

*bewail,* show grief with tears or cries of sorrow.

*bid* (v.), to order or request.

*bill* (of a bird), beak.

*bitter,* (1) harsh-tasting (e.g. beer): opposite to sweet; (2) feelings of anger, disappointment, etc. which are compared to this taste.

*blade,* (1) cutting side of a sword or knife; (2) flat, pointed leaf of grass.

*bless,* call on God to favour (someone); *blessed,* favoured by God; *blessedness,* the state of being favoured.

*blindworm,* little creature like a snake, but harmless; called "blind" because of its very small eyes.

*bliss,* perfect joy.

*boar,* wild male pig.

*bob,* move up and down suddenly.

*bog,* a piece of wet, muddy ground.

*bond,* a strict and binding agreement.

*bosom,* human breast; the place where love has its centre.

*bracelet,* band on the arm worn as an ornament.

*brag* (v.), boast.

*brake,* part of a wood with trees or bushes growing closely together.

*brawl,* noisy or violent quarrel.

*brief,* short.

*brier,* thorny bush.

*bristled,* with short, stiff hair (like a pig's).

*brook,* a small stream of water.

*buds,* flowers or leaves before they have opened.

## C

*calendar,* a list of the days in the month or year, special dates, etc.

*carcass* (*carcase*), dead body of an animal, or (insultingly) of a man.

*cards*, a game played with cards marked "ace" (one), numbers up to 10, and pictures of kings, queens and knaves.

*casement*, part of a large window which can be opened by itself.

*caw*, the sound made by a crow (q.v.).

*celestial*, heavenly.

*chamber*, room of a house.

*changeling*, child exchanged for another at birth (the fairies were believed to do this, leaving an "elf-child" for the human one).

*chant*, sing.

*chaplet*, flowers made into a chain and hung round the head or neck.

*chaste*, virtuous or pure in matters of love; *chastity*, such virtue or purity.

*cherry*, small fruit with a hard stone, often bright red in colour.

*chide*, to scold.

*chin*, front of the jaw beneath the mouth.

*chink*, small gap or hole.

*choice*, what has been chosen; act of choosing,

*chorus*, part of a song or poem which a number of people join in singing together.

*chronicle* (v.), to set down as a record for the future.

*churchyard*, ground next to a church where the dead are buried.

*churn* (v.), to beat or shake up milk in order to make butter.

*clamorous*, noisy.

*claw*, pointed nail of an animal's or bird's foot.

*cloister*, an enclosed place for walking in the garden of a convent (q.v.).

*clown*, fool in a play (originally, a simple country man).

*coat* (of arms), set of signs (often strange shapes of animals, birds, etc.) used by ancient families on their weapons and buildings, and arranged in the frame of a shield (see *heraldry*, *crest*).

*cobweb* (name of a fairy), web made by a spider.

*colt*, young horse.

*comedy*, amusing play with a happy ending (e.g. *A Midsummer Night's Dream*).

*comic*, connected with comedy; causing amusement.

*compass* (v.), go round in a circle.

*comprehend*, to include (with something already known); to understand.

*con*, learn "by heart".

*conceal*, hide (something).

*conceive* (1) to begin the bearing of a child; (2) begin to form an idea.

*concord*, agreement.

*confer*, talk over, consult together.

*congealed*, frozen.

*conjunction* (in —), together.

*consecrate*, make holy; *-ed*, holy and not to be used for ordinary purposes.

*consent* (v.), agree; (n.) permission.

*conspire*, to plot.

*constrain*, compel.

*contrive*, to find a way (to do something).

*convent*, religious house for nuns (q.v.).

*coronet*, a small crown.

*counsel*, (1) advice; (2) opinions or thoughts of one's own.

*counterfeit* (v.), to imitate, make a pretence of; (n) a copy or imitation.

# GLOSSARY

*couple* (v.), to form pairs, male and female.

*courteous,* behaving with courtesy (q.v.).

*courtesy,* good manners, especially in the treatment of a lady.

*cowslip,* small wild flower, yellow. in colour, with little red spots.

*cradle,* small bed for a baby; sleeping-place (III.i.26).

*cranny (crannied,* adj.), (see *chink*).

*crescent,* shape of the moon while growing to fullness, the pointed tips being its "horns".

*crest* (in heraldry), a design above the "shield" with its coat of arms (q.v.).

*crimson,* bright red.

*cross* (v.), to hinder.

*crow* (n.), kind of large black bird which feeds on rubbish and dead bodies.

*crystal,* fine glass, or whatever is as clear as glass.

*cuckoo,* kind of bird, seen in Europe in spring, with a cry which sounds like its name.

*cue* (in a play), last words of a speech, that serve as the sign for another actor to enter or speak,

*cur,* mean kind of dog; insulting word for a man.

*curtsy,* polite greeting by bending the knees and lowering the body; in this play probably a low bow.


# D

*dale,* a small valley.

*dame,* lady.

*damned,* condemned to everlasting punishment after death.

*dank,* damp right through.

*decease* (v.), die.

*deck* (v.), put ornaments on, make beautiful.

*defile* (v.), make dirty; put to shame.

*derision,* mockery, scorn.

*despise* (v.), scorn.

*destiny,* fate; a divine power which decides in advance what will happen.

*detest,* dislike very much.

*device,* plan, idea (III.i.13).

*devise* (v.), to plan, arrange.

*devour,* eat up hungrily.

*devout,* devoted in service (usually in a religious sense).

*dewberry,* kind of black berry eaten as a fruit.

*die* (n.), small stone or bone with six sides, numbered one to six, used in a game (plural, *dice*).

*dignity,* true worth which calls for respect.

*dine,* to eat dinner (main meal of the day).

*discharge* (v.), to complete a task or duty.

*discord,* noises which do not agree with one another.

*discourse* (v.), speak at length; (n.) speech.

*discretion,* wise caution; *at your d.,* at your choice.

*disdain,* scorn; *-ful,* scornful.

*disobey,* to refuse to obey; *disobedience,* act of refusing to obey.

*disparage,* to speak of a person or thing as of little value.

*dissemble,* to hide the truth (and so deceive).

*dissension,* disagreement, dispute.

*dissolve,* turn into liquid (as when ice melts).

*distil,* to draw out the essence of a flower for making scent.

*distracted,* confused almost to madness.

188

*ditty,* short song.

*divine,* belonging to God or the gods; god- or goddess-like.

*dolphin,* large animal living in the sea.

*dote* (on), love foolishly.

*dowager,* a woman who lives on land or property that belonged to her dead husband.

*dragon,* an imaginary monster, like a snake with wings.

*dread,* great fear; *-ful,* fearful, causing dread.

*drowsy,* sleepy.

*duchess,* wife of a duke.

*dwarf,* unnaturally small person or thing (opposite to *giant*); *-ish,* dwarf-like.

*dye* (n.), artificial colouring; (v.) to colour by artificial means.

**E**

*eglantine,* scented wild rose.

*elf* (pl. *elves*), a kind of small fairies, supposed to live in the woods.

*elm,* tall European tree.

*eloquence,* trained speech-making.

*elves,* see *elf.*

*enamoured* (of), in love with.

*enmity,* feeling as between enemies; hatred.

*enterprise,* piece of work or duty taken upon oneself.

*enthralled,* forced to submit or obey, as if charmed.

*entice,* attract or tempt someone to come.

*entreat,* ask very earnestly for, beg.

*epilogue,* speech at the end of a play.

*ere,* before.

*error,* mistake.

*espy,* set eyes on, see.

*esteem* (v.), consider as; (n.) opinion.

*exile* (v.), condemn a person to live away from his country or home.

*expound,* explain.

*extempore,* without preparation (from Latin).

**F**

*fable,* story not based upon facts.

*fall out with,* quarrel, break friendship with.

*fancy, fantasy,* wandering thoughts, especially of love.

*fate* (see *destiny*), divine power which decides the future.

*fawn,* show love in a humble, dog-like way.

*feign,* pretend.

*fellow,* companion; *fellowship:* company.

*fie,* shame on you!

*fig,* soft green or purple fruit, red inside; grows chiefly in Mediterranean countries.

*filch,* steal in a mean way.

*filly,* young female horse.

*finch,* kind of small bird.

*fled* (from *fly*), ran away.

*flight,* escape.

*flock,* number of sheep living and moving about together.

*flout,* mock at, show scorn for.

*flute,* (1) musical instrument played by being blown through; (2)stop of an organ (q.v.).

*fly,* run away, escape.

*foal,* young horse; (*filly foal,* a young female horse [mare]).

*fog,* thick mist.

*fold* (n.), an enclosed place for sheep.

*folly,* foolishness.

*forester,* a person who looks after or guards a forest.

*forsake* (past: *forsook*), give up, leave.

*forswear*, (1) swear to give up; (past, to have *forsworn*) (2) break one's pledge.

*fountain*, water springing out of a rock or side of a hill; a spring.

*fowler*, hunter of birds (*fowl*).

*fox*, small wild animal with a bushy tail, which feeds on chickens.

*fragrant*, sweet-smelling.

*frantic*, extremely excited.

*fray* (n.), fight.

*freckles*, little brown marks in the skin, usually of fair people.

*frenzy*, madness, great excitement.

*fruitless*, (1) without children; (2) without benefit.

*further*, more far.

## G

*gait*, way of walking.

*gallant*, brave and noble.

*gambol* (v.), run about like a child playing.

*gape* (v.), (1) to have the mouth wide open; (2) to be open wide (e.g. "a gaping hole").

*garlic*, plant with beard-like root, used in cooking; has a strong smell.

*garter*, band tying the stocking to the leg.

*giant*, unnaturally large person, animal or plant.

*girdle*, belt.

*glance* (v.), look quickly.

*gleam* (n.), faint beam of light.

*glide* (v.), move smoothly and silently.

*glimmer* (v.), shine faintly.

*glitter* (v.), shine brightly.

*glow-worm*, insect whose tail sends out a green light at night (in this play the light is believed to come from its eyes).

*goblin*, a spirit of mischief.

*gore*, blood grown thick.

*gossip* (v.), talk familiarly as between neighbours.

*grace* (your –), polite way of addressing a duke.

*gracious*, kind to those less powerful or important.

*graft* (v.), to put the stem of one plant in that of another, so that a new kind of plant grows up.

*grape*, small soft, round fruit growing in bunches on vines (q.v.); from the juice of it wine is made.

*griffin*, imaginary creature, half eagle, half lion.

*grim*, stern, cruel.

*gross* (-ness), coarse (ness).

*grove*, a small wood.

## H

*hail*, rain, frozen to ice, which falls in very cold weather; *hailstones*, frozen drops of hail.

*hail!*, a respectful greeting.

*hand* ( at –), near.

*hand* (in –), ready.

*handicraft*, skilled work with the hands; *handicraft man*, skilled worker.

*harelip*, a split in the middle of the upper lip, with which some children are born.

*harp*, musical instrument with strings.

*harsh*, rough or rude.

*haunted*, visited by ghosts.

*hawthorn*, thorny bush with scented pale flowers that open in England late in May.

*hawthorn-brake*, land thickly grown (see *brake*) with hawthorn bushes.

*hay*, dried grass as a food for horses and donkeys.

*hedgehog,* small, brown animal of the fields, with pointed nose and sharp thorny growths on its back, which stand up when it is disturbed.

*heel,* back part of the foot, raised when one runs.

*hemp,* a plant used for making rope and coarse cloth; *hempen,* made with hemp.

*heraldry,* the use of "coats of arms" and "crests" (q.v.) as a mark of nobility.

*herb,* useful plant for food, medicine or magic.

*heresy,* opinion about religion which is against the general belief.

*highness* (yours, his, etc.), respectful title for a ruler or prince.

*hindrance,* that which hinders.

*hip,* bone where top of the leg joins the body.

*hoard* (n.), store.

*hog,* pig.

*honey,* a sweet, yellow, eatable liquid made from flowers by bees.

*honey-bag,* part of the bee's body where the material for honey-making is stored.

*honeysuckle,* climbing plant with yellow, sweet-smelling flowers.

*hoot* (v.), make a loud, long noise (like the sound of this word).

*horn,* (1) hard growth on the head of some animals, used as a material for cups, cases, etc.; (2) an instrument for blowing through, making a loud sound.

*hound,* hunting dog.

*hue,* colour.

*humble-bee,* a large wild bee which makes a loud humming noise as it flies.

*hymn,* religious song.

## I

*imbrue,* to stain with blood.

*mpair,* weaken.

*inconstant,* changing in mind or behaviour.

*interchange,* exchange.

*interlude,* short play, of a kind that was already old-fashioned in Shakespeare's time.

*invisible,* not able to be seen.

*issue* (n.), children.

*ivy,* kind of plant that climbs round trees.

## J

*jest* (n.), a joke; (v.), to make a joke, cause amusement generally.

*joiner,* maker of light wooden furniture.

*jollity,* joyfulness.

*juggler,* (1) player of skilful tricks as entertainment; (2) a deceiver.

## K

*keen,* sharp, cruel.

*key* (in music), a set of musical sounds based on one note.

*kindred,* relations (members of a family).

*kinsman,* a relative.

*knave,* wicked person; *knavish,* wicked; *knavery,* wickedness.

*knight,* title given in the middle ages to brave noblemen, whose duty was to fight enemies of God and the king, and to protect ladies from attack and danger. Now given for many other reasons.

## GLOSSARY

### L

*lament* (v.), show grief for; *lamentable*, sad, regrettable.

*languish*, droop, lose strength.

*lantern*, lamp for carrying, with the flame covered by a case against wind or rain.

*lark*, a small brown bird with a beautiful song, which may be heard high in the sky at sunrise.

*late* (of –), lately, recently.

*leaden*, heavy or dull as lead.

*league*, (1) an old measure of distance, about 3 miles; (2) agreement.

*leathern*, made of, or looking like, leather.

*leek*, green plant tasting like an onion (q.v.), used to give flavour in cooking.

*leviathan*, supposed sea-creature, the biggest in the world (from the Bible).

*liar*, a teller of lies.

*lime*, kind of white earth made from limestone, used as a building material.

*lion*, wild animal, dark yellow in colour, very strong and fierce, found in Africa and parts of Asia, which attacks cattle and sometimes human beings.

*liquor*, liquid.

*loam*, wet clay mixed with sand for making plaster when building with bricks.

*loathe* (v.), dislike extremely; *loathing* (n.), extreme dislike.

*loth*, sorry.

*lull* (v.), put to sleep by gentle speech or sounds.

*lullaby*, a gentle song to lull a child to sleep.

*lunatic*, a madman; person whose mind is affected by the moon (Latin, *luna*).

*lurk*, lie in hiding.

### M

*maid*, maiden, unmarried girl; *maiden meditation*, thoughts fitting to a maiden.

*mantle*, loose coat without sleeves, worn by women.

*mar*, spoil; destroy.

*mare*, female horse.

*mark* (v.), take notice (of).

*marvel*, strange or wonderful thing or event; *marvellous*, strange, wonderful.

*mask*, a covering of cloth, or veil, over the face.

*masque*, kind of play which includes much music, song and fine scenery.

*maypole*, a tall post standing in an open place in English villages, painted in bright colours, round which country people have danced on May 1st since ancient times.

*meadow*, field or piece of grassland.

*meddle*, interfere.

*meditation*, deep thought.

*melancholy*, sadness as a habit of mind.

*melody*, tune in music.

*merchandise*, goods brought by merchants.

*mermaid* (sea-maid), imaginary creature, half-fish and half-maiden, supposed to live in the sea and sing very beautifully.

*merry*, cheerful.

*messenger*, carrier of messages.

*midst* (in the –), middle,

*mistress*, woman loved by a man.

*moan*, cry of pain or sorrow.

*mole*, brown mark on the skin at birth.

# GLOSSARY

*momentary*, lasting only for a moment.

*monster*, (1) animal of enormous size or unnatural shape; (2) a man who is unnatural in shape or behaviour.

*monstrous*, like a monster, unnatural; (*monstrous little voice*, an unnaturally low voice).

*moonbeam*, beam of light from the moon.

*mortal*, (1) any creature that must, in the end, die; (2) human being (as distinguished from fairies, gods, etc., supposed to be *immortal*, living for ever).

*moth* (name of a fairy), kind of insect that flies by night, especially around lamps and open flames.

*mould* (v.), to shape.

*mourn*, grieve for a death.

*mulberry*, whitish fruit of a tree, on the leaves of which silk-worms feed.

*munch*, eat as a horse or donkey does, with much use of the jaws.

*murrain* (murrion), sickness of animals.

*musk-rose*, a kind of climbing rose with a strong scent.

*mustard-seed* (name of a fairy), seed of the mustard plant, from which a hot-tasting yellow spice is made for eating with beef.

## N

*negligence*, neglect.

*neigh* (n.), noise made by a horse; (v.) to make this noise.

*newt*, small creature with a tail, found in rivers.

*nightingale*, a small bird famous for its beautiful singing, especially at night.

*nosegay*, bunch of scented flowers carried in the hand.

*notwithstanding*, in spite of; none the less.

*nowadays*, in these days, in our time.

*nun*, a woman who, for religious reasons, has sworn not to marry and to live simply and poorly under discipline in a convent (q.v.).

*nuptial*, wedding; (adj.) of a wedding.

*nymph*, spirit in the form of a beautiful maiden; flattering word for a girl.

## O

*oak*, a common kind of tree in northern countries; its fruit is the acorn (q.v.).

*oath*, a statement one swears to be true; or a promise made to God.

*oats*, kind of grain, grown in cold countries; eaten raw by animals.

*obedience*, the act or habit of obeying.

*oft*, often.

*onion*, plant with thick base used in cooking, which has a strong, sharp smell.

*order* (religious –), organization of persons under a religious discipline (order of monks, nuns, etc.).

*organ*, large musical instrument, often used in churches, played by pulling out different "stops" in the pipes.

*orient*, from the east; *orient pearl*, precious pearl.

*overhear*, hear what is said to another person and not intended for the listener.

*oxlip*, sweet-smelling wild flower, yellow, and rather like a cowslip (q.v.).

## P

*paragon*, person who is a model to others of all that is perfect.

*pare*, to cut (the finger or toe nails).

*part* (in play), that part of a play to be spoken or performed by a particular actor (e.g. Bottom takes the *part* of Pyramus).

*peaseblossom* (name of a fairy), flower of the pea.

*peck* (n.), large measure for corn.

*perceive*, see or realize with the mind.

*peril*, danger.

*perjure* (v.), to swear falsely.

*persever*(e), continue in a determined way with one's work or enterprise.

*pilgrimage*, journey made for religious reasons; used as an image of human life.

*pipes*, musical instruments played by blowing through pipes.

*play fellow*, companion in the play (games) of children.

*plead*, argue (a matter) for (someone).

*pluck*, pull off.

*potion*, drink of medicine, or poison.

*premeditated*, thought out beforehand.

*press*, urge, try to persuade (someone to do something).

*primrose*, plant with pale yellow flowers that open in early spring.

*privilege*, a special right enjoyed by some persons only.

*progeny*, children or descendants.

*prologue*, (1) a speech introducing a play; (2) the person making this speech.

*promontory*, point of high land stretching out into the sea.

*prove*, turn out to be, become.

*provender*, food (hay, etc.) for horses and donkeys.

*proverb*, a wise saying which is generally known and repeated.

*pumps*, light shoes (for dancing, etc.).

*purge* (v.), make pure, force out impurity.

## Q

*quake*, tremble, shake.

*quench*, put out fire with water.

*quern*, a small mill where corn is ground up to make flour.

*quill*, feather.

## R

*radiant*, bright, shining.

*rage* (n.), extreme anger.

*rash*, without heed; lacking in thought as to the results of words or acts.

*ravish*, carry off by force.

*rear* (up), bring up or train (a child).

*rebuke*, scold or speak sternly to, because of a fault committed.

*recompense*, reward.

*recorder*, musical instrument played by blowing through (a kind of flute [q.v.]).

*recount*, tell over, repeat.

*region*, large district, wide area of country.

*rehearse*, to practise acting a play; *rehearsal*: a practice performance of a play.

GLOSSARY

*relent,* become less stern and fixed in one's intentions.

*render,* give up (to).

*repent,* be sorry for, regret.

*report,* loud noise, as when a gun is fired.

*reprehend,* to find fault with, blame.

*restore,* give back; *restore amends,* put matters right again.

*revel* (v.), to make merry; (n.) merry-making, entertainment.

*revenue,* wealth from rents or profits.

*riddle* (v.), to speak in words with a hidden meaning; (n.) a puzzle in words.

*riot* (n.), disorderly or violent behaviour.

*rose,* a garden flower, usually red or white, with a pleasant scent, which grows on a thorny stem (briar).

*rough-cast,* a wet mixture made of sand and small stones, used in building.

*rush* (n.), plant with long stem growing by the water side; *rushy,* having rushes near by.

S

*sampler,* picture in needlework made to be hung up as a "sample" (example) of skill.

*satire,* kind of writing which attacks, or shows scorn for, people's faults and vices.

*saucy,* over-bold, disrespectful.

*savour,* smell of a pleasant kind.

*scandal,* that which causes public annoyance; or talk bringing others into disgrace.

*scar* (n.), a mark left by a wound.

*scare* (v.), frighten.

*screech* (n.), a high scream; *screech-owl,* kind of owl which makes this sound.

*script* (*scrip*), papers containing the words of a play or story.

*scroll,* sheet of paper rolled up.

*seething,* boiling; extremely excited.

*sentinel,* soldier on guard; sentry.

*serpent,* snake.

*shallow,* not deep (said also of a person's character).

*shears,* long scissors.

*shed* (tears), let tears fall from the eyes.

*shepherd,* keeper of sheep.

*shiver* (v.), shake from cold or fear.

*shower,* heavy fall of rain, hail, etc.

*shrew,* a scolding woman; *shrewish-ness,* scolding behaviour.

*shroud,* cloth in which a dead body is wrapped before burial.

*shun,* turn away from, avoid meeting.

*siege,* placing of enemy soldiers round a town or strong place, so that the defenders inside it are cut off from help; *lay siege to,* to attack slowly in this way.

*sigh,* deep breath taken as expressing sadness.

*signior,* master, sir. (Italian *signor.*)

*silly,* foolish.

*single,* not married.

*skim,* to take cream from the top of the milk.

*skip,* move quickly and lightly.

*sleek,* with smooth, bright hair.

*slumber* (v.), to sleep.

*snail,* small creeping animal that feeds on plants, with soft body and hard shell on its back, into which it draws its body when disturbed.

*snore* (v.), make noises through the nose or throat while sleeping.

*sound* (sleep –), deep; undisturbed.

*sovereignty*, highest authority; rule.

*spaniel*, a kind of dog, known as very affectionate and obedient.

*sparrow*, a small brown bird.

*spider*, eight-legged creature that spins or weaves a web to catch insects.

*sprite*, spirit.

*spurn*, kick out of one's way.

*squash*, kind of large climbing plant which can be cooked and eaten.

*squirrel*, small grey or reddish animal with a bushy tail that lives in trees and eats nuts.

*stab* (v.), to stick a knife into.

*state*, ceremony; *stately*, ceremonious, dignified.

*stature*, height of a person.

*steal* (away, forth), escape quietly.

*stool*, small seat with no back; *three-foot –*, stool with three legs.

*straightway*, immediately.

*stubborn*, unwilling to obey or come to an agreement.

*sunder*, to separate, cut apart.

*supper*, last meal at night.

*surfeit*, an excess, too large a quantity (usually of food eaten).

*surgeon*, doctor who performs operations.

*swagger*, walk in a bold, disrespectful manner.

*sway* (v.), to rule, control.

*sweetmeats*, sweets to be eaten.

*swift*, fast in moving.

*swoon*, to faint away.

*syllable*, part of a word, containing one vowel.

## T

*take* (the sense), understand.

*tale*, story.

*tangled*, confused and twisted in knots.

*taper*, small candle.

*task*, piece of work to be done.

*taunt* (v.), blame in a scornful way.

*tedious*, dull, wearying.

*tempest*, storm.

*temple* (of head), flat sides of the head above the ears.

*testy*, bad-tempered.

*thereof*, of it (the thing just mentioned).

*thistle*, thorny plant.

*thrice*, three times; very much (e.g. "thrice blessed").

*thyme*, sweet-smelling plant.

*tickle* (v.), to touch lightly with a hair, feather, etc., so as to irritate.

*tiger*, a large, fierce animal of the cat kind, with stripe markings, found in Asia.

*tinker*, mender of kettles, pans and other metal articles.

*title*, claim.

*toil*, hard work.

*token*, sign.

*topple*, fall over suddenly.

*torment* (v.), cause great pain or suffering to.

*tragedy*, play of a sad kind, usually with an unhappy ending.

*tragic(al)*, sad, distressing, as in a tragedy.

*train*, group of attendants who follow their master (or mistress).

*transpose*, change place with something else.

*trifle*, small article or thing of small value.

*troop* (v.), to march in company.

*turf*, piece of earth thickly grown with grass.

*tyrant*, a ruler, usually wicked or cruel. The tyrant was a common character in the "interludes" (q.v.).

## U

*undertake*, take upon oneself (to do something).

*unfold*, reveal, make clear.

*unhardened*, soft, gentle.

*upbraid*, blame, find fault with.

*utter*, speak out.

## V

*vain* (in –), with no result.

*valour*, courage.

*vexation*, annoyance.

*vile*, hateful.

*villain*, wicked man.

*vine*, plant on which grapes (q.v.) grow as fruit.

*visage*, face.

*vision*, something seen in a dream in imagination, or through supernatural means.

*vixen*, a she-fox (q.v.); a bad-tempered, quarrelsome girl or woman.

*votary*, *votaress* (f.), person who takes religious vows of service.

## W

*wane*, grow less; *in the* –, in the course of growing less.

*wanton*, (1) loose in behaviour; (2) playful.

*warrior*, fighter of wars.

*weep*, drop tears, "cry".

*wherefore*, why? for what reason?

*wit* (adj. *witty*), cleverness, good sense.

*withhold*, keep back.

*woe*, deep sorrow.

*womb*, part of the mother's body where the child grows.

*woo*, seek to marry, offer love to.

*woodbine* (see *honeysuckle*).

*wrath*, anger.

*wren*, a kind of small singing bird.

*wretch*, poor or unfortunate man; *wretchedness*, the condition of being poor or unfortunate.

## Y

*yawn* (v.), open the mouth wide as a result of being sleepy.

*yield* (v), to give up.

*yon*, *yonder*, over there, in the direction mentioned or pointed out.

# HINTS TO EXAMINATION CANDIDATES
## Prepared by H. M. Hulme, M.A., Ph.D.

This section is intended to offer some help to candidates who are studying *A Midsummer Night's Dream* for such examinations as School Certificate or the General Certificate of Education at Ordinary Level, and who are working alone. Actual questions from London papers are used as examples to show the kinds of question that may be found on most papers for examinations at this stage.

You will see first that you must know the story of the play in some detail. Secondly, you must give yourself practice in reading the questions carefully and answering exactly what is asked; *do not expect to find on any paper a question you have already answered*. Thirdly, you must train yourself to write quickly enough to finish the work in the time allowed (30 minutes for each of these sample questions). Do not waste time, for example, in copying out the question.

See to it that you know beforehand which kinds of question you *must* do and which you *may* do. For some examinations (e.g. London) you must do one "context" question and you may do also an essay question on the set play; for others (e.g. Cambridge) you may have some choice between "context" and essay questions.

### 'CONTEXT' QUESTION

Sample question from London University, G.C.E., Ordinary Level, Summer 1953.

1. Choose ONE of the following passages and answer the questions below it:

(i)

> So, at his sight, away his fellows fly,
> And, at our stamp, here o'er and o'er one falls;
> He murder cries, and help from Athens calls.
> Their sense thus weak, lost with their fears thus strong,
> Made senseless things begin to do them wrong;
> For briers and thorns at their apparel snatch;
> Some sleeves, some hats, from yielders all things catch.
> I led them on in this distracted fear,
> And left sweet Pyramus translated there.

(a) Who is the speaker and to whom is the speech addressed?
(b) State what happens immediately after this speech.
(c) Give the meaning in this passage of *from yielders all things catch* (l.7).
(d) Express in your own words the meaning of line four.
(e) Why does the speaker describe Pyramus as "sweet"?

(ii)

> Trust me, sweet,
> Out of this silence yet I picked a welcome;
> And in the modesty of fearful duty

> I read as much as from the rattling tongue
> Of saucy and audacious eloquence.
> Love, therefore, and tongue-tied simplicity
> In least speak most, to my capacity.

(a) Who is the speaker and to whom is the speech addressed?
(b) State what happens immediately before this speech.
(c) Give the meaning in this passage of *in the modesty of fearful duty* (l.3).
(d) Express in your own words what is meant by line seven.
(e) What light does the whole passage quoted above throw upon the character of the speaker?

*Notes on possible answers:*

Attempt one passage only.

Note that a good deal of accurate information is necessary here. Write as simply and shortly as possible. Number the sections carefully and see that you do not leave out any of the "bits", e.g. (i) (a) and (ii) (a) "to whom". Give only what, is asked e.g. (i) (b) *after*, (ii) (b) *before*.

The passage as given on the examination paper may be punctuated slightly differently from the passage as you know it. If so, follow the punctuation of the examination paper.

*Notes on* (i)

(a) Puck, Oberon.
(b) Demetrius tells Hermia that he loves her, but Hermia answers that she is afraid Demetrius has killed her love Lysander and she asks Demetrius never to see her again. Demetrius falls asleep and Oberon, thinking that Puck has made a mistake with the love-juice, orders him to bring Helena before the eyes of Demetrius as he wakes.
(c) Everything takes away the belongings of men who are willing to give them up. Because the Athenian workmen are willing to lose their sleeves and hats if only they can get away, it seems that the briers and thorns are tearing their clothes even more fiercely.
(d) Their power of reason, as feeble as I have described it, disappearing completely when they are so frightened at the sight of the ass's head. . . .
(e) In the rehearsal of the play Bottom, as Pyramus, speaks sweetly to Thisbe, his love.
Titania is so much in love with Bottom that she thinks he is an angel of sweetness.

(a) Give the names in the correct order.
(c) Do not use in your answer the words *yielders* or *catch* or any words formed from these.
(d) A question which begins "Express in your own words the meaning of" requires a neatly arranged answer which will make clear, by re-wording, the sense of *every* important word which is used: here *sense, thus, weak,*

200

lost, fears, thus, strong need to be taken into account. Do not use in your answer any of these given words or words formed from them, e.g. losing. Try out your attempt in pencil first; your final version should be written out clearly without any crossings out.

(e) Try to give two different points for this section.

*Notes on* (ii)

(a) Why would you get no marks for this answer: Hippolyta, Theseus ...?
(b) Note the instructions *immediately before*.
———insists on seeing the play "———"although ———warns him that ———. When ——— protests that she does not like to see poor hardworking men making fools of themselves in trying to please the Duke, ——— answers that he always has been more pleased when ——— who have practised speeches so as to ——— him have forgotten these speeches out of nervousness, thus showing their sincerity.
(c) Give a short phrase which would fit grammatically into the sentence so as to replace exactly the given words. Do not use in your answer the words *modesty, fearful,* or *duty,* or any words formed from these, e.g. *modest, full of fears, duteous.* Try out your attempt before looking at the answer given below.
(d) Why would you get no marks for the following answer? Genuine affection then and a natural feeling which cannot express itself in words. . . .
Why would you lose marks for the following?
In saying least express the most, as far as I am capable of judging. . . . ?
(e) Give two separate points.
Theseus shows his kindly nature when he understands the genuine affection shown to him by the man who is too nervous to remember his prepared speech.
He shows good judgement in preferring the humble affection of simple people to the rattling eloquence of those who are bold and insincere.

(a) See that you can spell the names correctly.
(c) In the shamefaced confusion shown by a true servant who is afraid of his ruler. . . .
(d) When they can scarcely say a word, yet they express the truest welcome, as far as I can understand.

ESSAY QUESTION
Sample questions from London University, G.C.E. Ordinary Level, Summer 1953.

1. What impression do you get of the Athenian artisans (excluding Bottom) from their speeches and actions (a) during the preparation of their play and (b) during its performance before the Duke?

2. Write a brief account of (a) the quarrel between Titania and Oberon, and (b) the quarrel between Hermia and Helena, commenting on the contrast

between the language of the two fairies and that of the two mortals in these quarrels.

Each of these questions requires *detailed knowledge* of the play. Make some *brief notes* before you begin to write. Remember that you will certainly not have time to write out the whole essay in rough and then copy it out later. Plan carefully; the way in which the question is arranged will tell you how to plan your answer.

Any quotations given should be short; do not waste time on long quotations of ten or twenty lines; it is more important to show that you can yourself write simply and clearly. When quoting poetry, quote in lines and begin the quotation about one inch from the left-hand margin. The quotations given should fit grammatically into your own sentences.

*Notes on possible answers:*

*Question 1*

*Plan*

As the question is set in two sections (*a*) and (*b*), write your answer in two sections, giving, if you wish, slightly more than half your time to (*b*) since the *performance* of the play is more important than the *preparation* for it.

In each section give roughly one third of your attention to *speeches*, one third to *actions* and one third to your *impression* of these. It is not necessary to write separate paragraphs under these headings.

*Material*

(*a*) *preparation of their play* Act. I, Sc. ii (pp. 21–9), Act. III, Sc. ill. 1–86 (pp. 63–71), Act IV, Sc. ii ll. 1–26 (pp. 143–5).

(*b*) *performance* Act. V, ll 108–335 (pp. 155–177).

No marks will be given for speeches or actions of Bottom (and therefore of Pyramus). Do not spend your time on the speeches of any other characters who watch the play prepared or performed.

*Arrangement*

(*a*) For a good answer, include five or six of these or similar points and one or two short quotations:

at the first meeting of the company: Quince enjoys organising, disposes of practical difficulties: Flute, who "has a beard coming" can play in a mask, Snug who is afraid that he cannot learn the lion's part quickly enough "may do it extempore for it is nothing but roaring". We believe in their artless plan and sympathize with the simple actors.

at the rehearsal in the wood: the details seem real; Quince speaks of "this hawthorn-brake, our tiring-house". Snout and Starveling are timid; one says "We must leave the killing out", the other asks "Will not the ladies be afeard of the lion?" Quince decides that an actor may come in "to disfigure, or to present, the person of Moonshine. . . ."

202

at Quince's house: Quince speaks of a "paramour" instead of a "paragon" (This scene could be left out if you have enough material without it.)

(b) For a good answer give five or six brief points and one or two short quotations.

As the Prologue, Quince misplaces the punctuation so that the meaning is spoilt:

All for your delight
We are not here!

He tells the audience all the story of the play. He tries to use impressive and poetical language. Snout carries building material to show that he is a wall and gives his real name also. Thisbe kisses the chink of the wall with her "cherry lips". (You will see from this beginning what kind of points to choose. Bring out the fact that the workmen are quite serious in all they do.)

Begin to write without any introduction using some of the words of the question: We (or I) get the impression that the Athenian artisans are real people and sympathize with their simplicity as they meet to prepare their play.

## Question 2

### Plan

It is possible to plan an answer in two sections (a) and (b) giving comment on the *contrast between the language* while you are describing the quarrels. But since at least one third of the marks will be given for the *contrast* section it will be far better to deal with this in a separate third paragraph.

### Material

(a) the quarrel between Titania and Oberon: Act II, Sc. i ll. 60–145 (pp. 34–41).
(b) the quarrel between Hermia and Helena: Act III Sc. ii ll. 191–343 (pp. 97–111).

### Arrangement

For a good answer try to give three points in each of the sections (a) and (b) together with some short quotations. Be careful to keep back some short quotations for your third *contrast* paragraph.

(a) Titania is jealous that Oberon has come "from the farthest steppe of India" to give joy and prosperity to his mistress Hippolyta who is to be married to Duke Theseus of Athens. Oberon answers that he knows that Titania loves Theseus.
Titania is sorry that her fairy dances are spoiled by Oberon's quarrel with her and that the climate of the changing seasons has been spoiled for human mortals.

Oberon asks Titania for the little changeling boy. Titania refuses to give up the child but asks Oberon to dance in her "moonlight revels".

(b) Lysander and ——— both declare their love for ———, and she believes that Hermia is joining with the young men to mock her. She ——— Hermia of their ——— as children and thinks that Hermia is only ———not to understand her reproaches.

Hermia thinks at first that ——— is still in love with her. When she realizes that he is not, she is angry with ——— for stealing her "love's heart" and is ready to strike her.

Hermia is convinced that Helena is proud of being the taller of the two.

## "Contrast" paragraph

The "contrast" is the "difference between". See that you read the question carefully and deal only with *the contrast between the language*. No marks will be given for contrast between the characters or their actions. Try to find two or three good points, e.g.:

Although the fairies are angry, they speak to each other with calmness and royal self-command: "proud Titania" "jealous Oberon". The mortals, by contrast, abuse each other as "puppet" and "painted maypole".

Titania leaves Oberon so that they shall not "chide downright". As the mortals quarrel, Hermia is so lacking in self-control that she threatens to scratch out Helena's eyes.

The mortals are so childish in their anger that their language makes us laugh. The language of the fairies is poetic. Titania speaks of the "beached margent of the sea" and Oberon of the "glimmering night".

Additional questions, from London University, G.C.E., Ordinary Level, Autumn 1952.

1. Choose one of the following passages and answer the questions below it.

(i)

> Things base and vile, holding no quantity,
> Love can transpose to form and dignity,
> Love looks not with the eyes but with the mind,
> And therefore is wing'd Cupid painted blind.
> Nor hath Love's mind of any judgement taste;
> Wings and no eyes figure unheedy haste;
> And therefore is Love said to be a child,
> Because in choice he is so oft beguil'd.

(a) Who is the speaker and to whom is the speech addressed?
(b) State what happens immediately before this speech.
(c) Give the meaning in this passage of *figure* (l.6) and *beguil'd* (l.8).
(d) Put line 5 into your own words.
(e) What light does this passage throw upon the character of the speaker?

## (ii)

More strange than true. I never may believe
These antique fables, nor these fairy toys.
Lovers and madmen have such seething brains,
Such shaping fantasies, that apprehend,
More than cool reason ever comprehends.
The lunatic, the lover, and the poet,
Are of imagination all compact.

(a) Who is the speaker and to whom is the speech addressed?
(b) State what happens immediately before this speech.
(c) Give the meaning in this passage of *fairy toys* (l.2) and *compact* (l.7).
(d) Put lines 4 and 5 into your own words.
(e) What light does this passage throw upon the character of the speaker?

2. Give an account of the characteristics of Puck as revealed by (a) the conversation early in the play between him and the unnamed fairy and (b) his dealings with the lovers.

3. What impressions have you formed of the Athenian workmen from (a) the rehearsals for their play and (b) the final performance of their play? Notice carefully how the material required to answer this question is different from that required for the first essay question given above.

4. What do you learn of Shakespeare's knowledge of the countryside from references in the play to (a) country customs and (b) country scenes and creatures.

5. By considering their speeches and actions (a) which fairies would you say are most fairy-like and (b) which fairies most like human beings?